Going to See
the Elephant

OTHER BOOKS BY GEORGE GARRETT

Fiction

King of the Mountain
The Finished Man
Which Ones Are the Enemy?
In the Briar Patch
Cold Ground Was My Bed Last Night
Do, Lord, Remember Me
A Wreath for Garibaldi
Death of the Fox
The Magic Striptease
The Succession
An Evening Performance
Poison Pen
Entered from the Sun
The Old Army Game
The King of Babylon Shall Not Come Against You

Poetry

The Reverend Ghost: Poems
The Sleeping Gypsy and Other Poems
Abraham's Knife and Other Poems
For a Bitter Season: New and Selected Poems
Welcome to the Medicine Show
Luck's Shining Child
The Collected Poems of George Garrett
Days of Our Lives Lie in Fragments

Plays

Sir Slob and the Princess
Enchanted Ground

Nonfiction and Compilations

James Jones
Understanding Mary Lee Settle
The Sorrows of Fat City
That's What I Like (About the South: And Other New
Southern Stories for the Nineties)
Whistling in the Dark
My Silk Purse and Yours
Bad Man Blues: A Portable George Garrett

Going to See the Elephant

PIECES OF A WRITING LIFE

George Garrett

Edited by Jeb Livingood

TEXAS REVIEW PRESS
Huntsville, Texas

Requests for permission to reproduce material
from this work should be sent to:

Permissions
Texas Review Press
English Department
Sam Houston State University
Huntsville, TX 77341-2146

Cover photograph: Patrick Cribben
Cover design: Kellye Sanford

Versions of some of these pieces have appeared in magazines including
*Callaloo, Chattahoochie Review, Chronicles, Idaho Review, The
Observer, Ploughshares, and The Virginia Quarterly Review;* and in an-
thologies including *Creating Fiction, Eudora Welty: Writers'
Reflections Upon First Reading Eudora Welty, F. Scott Fitzgerald: New
Perspectives, A Goyen Companion, Letters to a Fiction Writer,* and *The
Professions of Authorship.*

LIBRARY OF CONGRESS CATALOGING-IN-PUBLICATION DATA

Garrett, George P., 1929–
　　Going to see the elephant : pieces of a writing life / George Garrett ;
　　　edited by Jeb Livingood.
　　　　p. cm.
　　ISBN 1-881515-42-7 (pbk. : alk. paper)
　　　1. Garrett, George P., 1929–　2. Authors, American—20th century—
　　　Biography. 3. Authorship. I. Livingood, Jeb. II. Title

PS 3557.A72 Z465 2002
818'.5409—dc21
[B]　　　　　　　　　　　　　　　　　　　　　2001027801

Printed in the United States of America

For Jill and Samuel
—J.L.

For all my students over the many years
—G.G.

Language enables us to take pieces of our lived time, and to move them out of time into the form of what Borges always called a "fiction"—poems, essays, stories, they are all fictions.
—Alastair Reid, "Borges Beyond Words"

I realize as clearly as anyone else how unseemly it is for a writer to be anything but insouciant about book reviews, publicity, and sales figures.
—Tom Wolfe, "My Three Stooges"

"By God, I tell you the literary life's the thing," Pop said. "You can't beat it!"
—Ernest Hemingway, *Green Hills of Africa*

Contents

II. Other Voices

III. True and False Confessions

Introduction

BY JEB LIVINGOOD

There is art, the kind that makes a statement or captures an emotion, and then there is the *art*—often appearing at the most unexpected places and times—that stays with you forever.

In 1982, when I first saw Gutzon Borglum's statue "The Aviator," it had that sort of impact. There it stood, the awkward and tilting likeness of James R. McConnell, a dark patina on the wings and bare chest, the tense face turned toward the clouds. I was a new first-year student at the University of Virginia (in body, as awkward and tilting as the statue) and stared at the likeness of an alumnus about whom I knew next to nothing. And yet, looking at that weather-worn bronze, that representation of a man long dead, it seemed as though I already knew what mattered most.

The McConnell statue has hardly remained fixed over the years, has, in fact, flittered around the university's grounds like a swallow. The construction of a new (now old) gymnasium and a new (now expanding) library pushed the bronze McConnell to ever-changing vantages. It currently rests on a walkway outside of the undergraduate library, a building where, among other things, you can check out the movie *Gladiator* on DVD for a period of not more than three days.

As it should be. The statue, that is.

For the statue of McConnell stands there, I think, to provide a glimpse of a life almost unimaginable to most University of Virginia students. After all, how many of them can relate to a man who voluntarily served under France's flag in "The War to End All Wars" because his own country had yet to commit? Even after the tragedies of September 11, 2001, the notion of fighting for a foreign cause, especially one that has yet to threaten the United States directly, would seem a sort of romantic foolishness to many undergraduates, perhaps an unnecessary intervention to others. And yet history has largely been on McConnell's side, even if that history has become little more than a whisper in our world of CNN footage and movie violence. A fleeting history then, one quickly forgotten or only dimly recalled.

In the classroom, I was reminded of the great speed at which this can happen when I asked my composition students to describe Judith Ortiz Cofer's short-short story "Kennedy in the Barrio." A bright young woman said, "Oh, when that little girl hears about the Kennedy assassination, it's like one of those events you only remember because your parents told you about it. You know, the fall of the Berlin Wall or something."

I nearly fell over as well. But there they were, eighteen first-year college students who might never fully appreciate a piece of history that changed my world—and theirs—forever.

Then again, I never really considered myself all that separate from the writers who came before me, writers like George Garrett. Yet as Garrett makes perfectly clear in these pages, not only do different generations of writers have trouble fully understanding each other, we may, in fact, be unable to do so at all. In describing the masters of his own literary apprenticeship—Joyce, Proust, and Mann; Hemingway, Fitzgerald, and Faulkner; Pound and Eliot—Garrett writes, "We simply imagined ourselves to be younger and maybe less-gifted versions of these people, living in roughly the same world and working under roughly the same conditions, able, therefore, to profit directly by and from their examples and, indeed, able to learn many practical things from them." He later concludes, "Years of hard experience have taught me that we were wrong about all this; in truth, we live in a radically different world from that of the earlier generation of modern masters."

Garrett also warns—in both his own voice and that of his fictional antithesis, John Towne—that the relatively new marriage of academia and creative writing and the ever-growing influence of popular culture can hardly be considered innocuous when it comes to contemporary literature. Who knows what such an emphasis on fame and celebrity will bring?

As Garrett tells us in his first essay, "Like it or not, the times they are a-changing all the time."

Still, I'd argue that a young writer can turn to George Garrett's quiet life by the pen—author of thirty-two books and editor or coeditor of nineteen—and glimpse, however briefly, a sense of the man, and perhaps more importantly, a sense of what it means to be a writer. Not technique, not how-to, but the profession's duties and obligations, its ultimate need for truth. Because, in the end, the writer's works have to stand on their own, naked and subject to the shifting winds, and like that statue of James R. McConnell, always reaching out, if only to one person at a time.

A Writing Life

Going to See the Elephant: Our Duty as Storytellers

There is magic and mystery at the heart of it. Say anything you want about "the creative process," but what is clear and certain is that we don't really understand it. It breaks all the rules as fast as we can make them. Every generalization about it turns out to be at best incomplete or inadequate.

Yet the making, the discovery that becomes the first draft of your story or mine, is what we most want to think about, to talk about, to teach and to learn. We copy the rituals, the ways and means of the masters, hoping somehow to plug into the circuits of their mastery. Did Thornton Wilder sharpen dozens of pencils to begin his day's work? I'll try it. Did Hart Crane play classical music on his record player as he tried to compose *The Bridge*? Why not? Did Ernest Hemingway really stop writing each day only if and when he was absolutely certain what the next sentence would be? Did William Faulkner really write *As I Lay Dying* in six weeks flat, front to back, in longhand on the bottom of an upside-down wheelbarrow and never thereafter change a word? (Well, as we know now, not exactly. A bit of a stretch.) Did Truman Capote write his "dark" books in the wee hours of the night and his more cheerful works in the morning? Maybe that will work for you . . . or me.

Truth is, we don't know what will work for us until we take the breathless plunge, until we follow the original impulse to wherever it tries to take us. "Trust your original impulse," I tell my students. Your muse may fool you and tease you sometimes, lead you on merry chases, but you must nevertheless learn to trust the muse and take the risks. Without that trust and that risk—nothing. Nothing new or worthy or admirable or . . . true. With the blessing of the muse (speaking through the language of your original impulse, however vague and inchoate), you can sometimes do wonderful things.

Do you know the story of the first poet in the English language? It's a lovely story told in Bede's *Ecclesiastical History of the English People*, maybe a factually correct story and maybe not, but certainly true in the sense we are talking about. Caedmon was an illiterate cowherd who worked at a monastery. In the evening in the refectory, when the monks and workers sat down to supper, they would pass a stringed instrument, a harp that was a kind of precursor to the guitar, around the table. And everybody would pluck a few chords and sing or recite some verses. And, seeing the harp coming his way, Caedmon would always sneak off, tiptoeing out to the barn where he slept in the hay with the farm animals all around. Caedmon was all thumbs when it came to playing the harp, and he didn't know any verses.

One night he was sound asleep in the barn when an angel appeared out of the cloudy nowhere angels come from and woke him. Caedmon was dazed in humility and awe and fear.

"Caedmon," the angel said. "Sing for me."

As politely as possible, Caedmon reminded the angel of what the supernatural being must already know—that he couldn't sing a note and didn't know any verses and that was why he was here, alone in the barn, while the supper's evening festivities were still going on.

The angel wasn't having any. "Nevertheless you will sing for me."

"What shall I sing?"

"Sing me the story of the Creation."

And, as if by miracle, words came into Caedmon's head and he sang (or recited) a little poem about the creation of the world. Look it up sometime, the earliest known poem in the English language, therefore the earliest official poet in the English language.

The elements of the story are worth mentioning. The key, the trigger, the source, of course, was the angel. No angel and no poem. Is that the same angel that Wallace Stevens had in mind (among many other things) when he called his book of essays about the art of poetry *The Necessary Angel?* Note that the first poem in our language, brief as it is, told a story. Storytellers are poets, also, even if they, mostly, don't tell their stories in verse. Bede tells us that Caedmon became a poet. The intellectual monks read him the Bible and other books, and he turned what he had learned from them and from his life into poetry (something none of them could do). Bede tells us Caedmon had a long life and a good one and died quietly.

We have to learn to wait for the angel to come to us. We have to be ready. The readiness is all. We have to believe in the magic and the mystery.

⊷══◉◉══⊷

Classes and workshops can't teach us much about the mysteries of inspiration, only some of the ancient exercises and rituals that worked for others. The teacher is supposed to know them and to pass them on. But beyond that, once you have felt an undeniable impulse and made your first draft, be it ever so sketchy and clumsy, beyond the vision, then, we can share with each other, teach and learn some of the many kinds of revision that can allow an original vision to arrive at its full power and glory and clarity. The special thing about creative writing classes and workshops is that we're all in this together, students and teachers; we're all in the same boat. And that is the great pleasure of it for the teacher, for what I've been doing since my first teaching job in 1956. There are plenty of things to pass along, plain practical matters and personal experiences. But the teacher and the student are equally focused on the same problems, and there are no permanent answers. Nothing is unbreakable bronze or stone. Everything, the world, is up for grabs. I think this is what some of the great teachers of creative writing really mean when they say (as they do), "I love teaching. It keeps me young." The great poet William Butler Yeats put it another way: "I now can but share with a friend my thoughts and emotions, and there is a continual discovery of difference, but in those days, before I had found myself, we could share adventures." A good workshop is a shared adventure.

⊷═◉ ◉═⊷

I once met a man who had spent some years living with and among the Pygmies in what is now Uganda. They are a fascinating people who have managed to survive in a very hostile environment and under most difficult circumstances. They have a complex language, a *click* language mastered and known by only a very few people outside their group. The man I met had never fully mastered their language, but he could talk and listen. So I asked him, "What kinds of things do they talk about?"

"The usual things," he shrugged.

Myself, persistent: "Anything unusual? Special?"

"Well, yes," he said. "There is one thing I ought to mention." And he went on to tell me that from early childhood to old age, Pygmies are uniformly comedians, stand-up comics. They tell great jokes. They tell jokes about everything. It's possible (Who knows?) that he, the expert, was having a little joke at my expense. For sure, he couldn't remember any Pygmy jokes to tell me. But I like to believe, until proved otherwise, that he spoke the factual truth, that these people, living their lives far from the sound and fury of the rest of the world, deep in the camouflage and secrecy of a great rain forest, have come to terms with the absurdity of the human condition, which they fully share, by becoming a race of jokers, stand-up storytellers for whom laughter is the truly appropriate response to what the world has to offer them or to take away. Sometimes I allow myself to imagine that, come the apocalypse we still half-expect to arrive at any time, the Pygmies alone will survive to begin the human race all over again. Our proper elegy and requiem will turn out to be a joke in a *click* language.

We should be so lucky.

Meanwhile, though, I am thinking of the Pygmies as an emblem of us and for us, of our art and craft as storytellers. Years ago I saw a documentary film about the Pygmies. One of the things the film showed was a hunting party that had managed to kill an elephant, thus bringing home enough meat to last them for a long time. The occasion called for a feast, where there was a reenactment of the hunt. What was wonderful about this reenactment, something that confirmed the story the expert had told me, was that the hunters, now as actors playing themselves, introduced a good deal of comedy into the story. For the Pygmies, armed with spears and blowguns, an elephant is a formidable and dangerous prey. Most of the time the elephant wins at the expense of any number of hunters. And this particular time had evidently been a close call for the hunters. The hunter-players showed that clearly enough, but through comedy. The imaginary elephant would lunge at them and, to the laughter and amusement of the audience, the hunters would throw away their weapons and hightail it to safety. The hunters were all heroes, but in performing the story they seemed to enjoy showing that at least some of them were heroes in spite of themselves. Perhaps if the hunt had ended in failure, the documentary would have shown us a Pygmy tragedy (if such a thing exists). But since the hunt went well (only one man had been slightly injured, and he played his part to laughter by exaggerating his injuries), it was an all's-well-that-ends-well comedy.

At the moment, sharing the double experience, the hunt and the reenactment, with them, I understood something about our duty and function as storytellers. It is up to us to tell the story of the hunt (event, experience, quest) as honestly and as accurately as possible, thus to call up and to appeal to the emotions of our audience (one reader at a time). Whether the audience is moved to laughter or tears depends on how it came to pass, in success or in failure. That is our currency as hunter-players, the universal coinage of laughter and tears.

Seeing this film about the Pygmies I was reminded of something the novelist and historian Shelby Foote once told me. He said that in the Civil War, veterans used to tell green recruits who were going into battle for the first time that they were "going to see the elephant." Bear in mind that few, if any, of these farm boys from the North and the South could have ever seen a living elephant in fact or in the flesh: the great traveling circuses came later in the century. It was a bad joke, whether any recruits believed it briefly or not. But it had a deep truth. Ever since Homer, storytellers trying to tell war stories have justly complained that the experience of combat is unimaginable to those who have not experienced it and, thus, finally, no matter how accurately rendered, inde-scribable, incommunicable. Writing about the battles in Western Europe in November and December of 1944, Stephen E. Ambrose (in *Citizen Soldiers*) adds the stipulation that the experience of combat cannot be prepared for.

> Every rifle company coming on the line that November had a similar experience and drew the same conclusion: there was no way training could prepare a man for combat. Combat could only be experienced, not played at. Training was critical to getting the men into physical condition, to obey orders, to use their weapons, to work efficiently with hand signals and radios, and more. It could not teach men how to lie helpless under a shower of shrapnel in a field criss-crossed by machine-gun fire. They just had to do it, and in doing it they joined a unique group of men who have experienced what the rest of us cannot imagine.

Thus the Civil War metaphor—"going to see the elephant." You are about to be introduced to something previously unimagined and unimaginable. The experience will change you forever.

Both of the above elephants, the "real" one from the Pygmy drama and the imaginary one from the Civil War, have something to do with what we do, our ancient and honorable task as storytellers. So does the familiar story of the three blind men, each of whom touched and examined part of an elephant and reported his finding. One touched the body of the elephant and declared that it was a great wall. Another touched the trunk and reported that it was a huge snake. The third touched the tail and called it a piece of rope. All three were, of course, right. An elephant is, indeed, all these things and more. It all depends—and every storyteller knows this—on your point of view. And your point of view—Pygmy, Civil War soldier, blind man—is always limited.

May I add one more brief, mildly irrelevant, personal elephant anecdote about which I can at least claim that it is true and it really happened to me?

Once when I was teaching at Bennington College in Vermont, I received an invitation secondhand from the college telephone operator. She told me that the poet and professor at Brown University, Michael Harper, had called and left a message for me, inviting me to come to Brown and participate in an elephant festival there. I prepared for the event by going to the library and reading up on elephants and even learning a few elephant jokes. When I took the Greyhound bus to Brown, I felt I was ready to be an active participant in the festival. When I stepped off the bus, there was Michael Harper standing by to greet me; and standing with him, smiling a welcome, was our mutual old friend, Ralph Ellison. *Ellison! Oh my God, it was an Ellison festival . . . !*

There has got to be a moral for writers somewhere, earned and illustrated by that anecdote. Don't depend on secondhand information—something like that. Somehow I managed to tell all the elephant jokes I had learned before the weekend was over and done with (*waste not, want not*). Other people must have thought I was obsessed with the subject. I never asked.

If we elders, veterans who have been to see the real-and-imaginary elephant, can't tell you much about the mystery and the magic, the secret initial (first draft) process of storytelling, what can we honestly and honorably tell you?

One of the first things I tell my students is a word or two about the literary past—how to live with it and how to use it. First of all, the past is simultaneous. That is, for the writer (for yourself as a writer, not as critic or reader), our literary past, our literary traditions and history, is not strictly chronological or evolutionary. Forms change and fashions come and go; habits are acquired and then are played out. But, for us writers, Homer and Virgil, Dante and Shakespeare and Hemingway are simultaneously past and can be, here and now, equally influential. They all have some lessons to teach us. Secondly, there is the related problem that none of us knows enough about our literary past or, indeed, about our time, the literary present. None of us, not you and not I, reads as much and knows as much as we ought to. I do not mean the weight of knowledge that could, if allowed, stifle or even silence us. Not by any means. Our studying, our reading of the past and the present, of the great ghosts and of each other, should liberate us. Unless we are willing to labor to know as much as we possibly can of our literary history and tradition, we are likely to be condemned to reinventing the wheel and the sail.

As to the present, in one sense that is even more important. Like it or not, the times they are a-changing all the time. We owe it to ourselves and to whatever gifts and talents we possess to appreciate and to try to understand the best that our contemporaries have already achieved. Judging by myself, and by my students, past and present, I conclude that we are all too often too ignorant for our own good. A primary generalization then: Unless you love to read and unless you read as much as you are able to, frivolously as well as wisely and well, you will not amount to much as a writer.

It is the burden of all of us, here and now, to know (as best we can) what we are up to. *We have to be more self-conscious than we usually are.* I do not mean to encourage this kind of sophistication and self-consciousness in the process and act of creation, the first searching draft and vision. Remember (as I said before) that after vision comes revision. You need to feel that during revision you can fix anything, change things to suit yourself. Revision is really what we are talking about in all of our classes and workshops.

A general word or two about what we try to do in revision. We always try to tell the truth, but we deal with the ways and means of seeming. No good story is really inevitable, first word to last. It only seems to be so, and that seeming comes from your skill and your authority. Use your authority to make your story seem absolutely inevitable even though you are fully aware that it is a sequence of choices and compromises powered by an original impulse. Be true to that impulse. But also, in revision, be as sly, cunning, crafty as you need to be.

⊷══◉══⊷

And now a couple of practical suggestions about the craft of storytelling, truths that I came to realize slowly, the hard way. Therefore, I am eager to share them, obvious as they may well be.

The fuel of all good narrative is suspense. The goal is forward motion. Coaches tell runners not to look back, because in a race you can lose a full step and more and break your running rhythm by trying to peek over your shoulder. A story is a run for it, a race without any serious interruption. Suspense is not merely a matter of what happens next; it is also a series of tantalizing questions. And it is not only a conflict between the ways of showing and the habits of telling. *Of course* we always want to dramatize as much as possible, to let the reader, engaged in the flow of imagined experience that is narrative, infer and discover. But we also have to find expeditious ways to *tell*. Show what you can and have to, and tell what you must, but do so, in both cases, with suspense in mind. Let the reader hurry along to keep up with you. Don't tell any more than you have to, and don't tell anything until you have to. Exposition is the area of craft where beginners and amateurs, even gifted ones, are most likely to stumble.

A little general rule worth considering is that when the story, by plot or the nature of its material, has built-in suspense, the less you have to impose suspense on it. And (maybe more important) vice versa.

If your story does not have a whole lot of inherent suspense, you can tell it the way the comics do when they tell a shaggy dog story: divert attention with details.

All of the above suggestions add up to the real necessity, at some point, of discovering and knowing the essential nature of your story. It is urgently important that you should know the kinds of feelings your story will summon up from a receptive and sympathetic reader. You must be that reader even as you write.

If suspense is the fuel that all narrative runs on, then repetition and redundancy are the chief causes of breakdown. Make a point, only one time if that is possible, then move on to the next one. Don't repeat yourself if you can help it. If you discover, while rereading and revising, that you have made the same point more than once, this usually indicates you haven't yet found the place where the point belongs.

Writing is an art as well as a craft. What defines any art is that it is, first and foremost, a sensuous, affective experience. This means that what happens between you and your reader is the evocation and engagement of the senses. That engagement is just as important, maybe more so, as the details of plot, action, character, structure. You must, first of all, convince your reader that your story, whether it pretends to be "real" or professes to be the purest fantasy, is sensuously perceptive. Use all five senses as early and as often as possible. Somehow this sensory sleight of hand becomes part of the magic spell that makes everything else work.

Another soapbox I like to stand on: Once you understand the story you are telling and what it seems to be about, try to go against the grain of it, in revision, as much as you can. For example, give a "bad" character some "good" traits. Similarly, give the good guys some bad habits. This won't change your story, or the point of it, but it will give your characters more dimension and complexity.

Your greatest, deepest choice as a storyteller, once you understand your story, is whether or not to go with the grain of it, to follow the expectations that the subject raises or to take the reader in another direction—the direction John Keats advocated when he said that poetry should surprise us with a "fine excess." Surprise is almost as important as suspense in storytelling. You must recognize that, as an artist, your chief enemy is the easy stereotype. Any stereotype. To create something new and worthwhile, to surprise by "a fine excess," question all stereotypes, good ones and bad ones, and the shadow assumptions behind them. Turn the full force of your own doubts and skepticism against the commonplace assumptions of your age and, most especially, against your own personal certainties and assumptions.

It is, to be sure, a gamble, a real risk every time. Go back to those Pygmy hunters for a moment. When the meat runs out, they must go hunting, risking life and limb, again and again. And then, for the sake of their fellows and their tribe, they have to reenact the experience of the hunt. That is what we do, too. As storytellers we are reenactors. We are called to an ancient and honorable enterprise, at least as old and probably older than the paintings on the walls of caves where our ancestors (of all shapes and sizes and colors) painted pictures to illustrate their stories and rituals. Learn your craft by any and all means, I tell the students in workshop. Then practice it with all the art and magic you can muster. Be worthy of your vocation, which is, after all is said and done, truly a career of danger and daring.

All that we can do, day by day, is share with each other some bits and pieces, fragments of guidance and understanding, which we have managed to acquire. We do the work alone, as alone as can be. ("Nobody else can take a bath for you," as the existentialists used to say.) But there is much that we can tell each other and much to be gained by sharing our experiences. We must work together to be ready, one at a time, for the necessary angel to arrive on the scene and the mystery and magic of making to begin.

A Writing Life

To the best of my sometimes cloudy recollection, I wanted to be a writer all my life. Even before I could read or write. Or course I didn't know, didn't have a clue what that meant, what was involved in being a writer or what writers did in real life. And I'm not sure I know now after almost fifty years of professional writing. I can look back now and see some things, patterns in how things happened, and even identify some misapprehensions that were based on faulty assumptions and on the absence of accurate information and on the prevalence of inapplicable myths. Most of these things I did not notice at the time, being, like so many of us, too busy with trivial things to take long views.

Let me start over.

I didn't quite tell the truth when I said I didn't have a clue what it was all about. Actually I did. I had clues and signs about the writing life, but I lacked the capacity to understand them. For one thing, I had before me the example of several writers in our family. One of them, on the Southern side of the family, was Harry Stillwell Edwards of Macon, Georgia. Hardly a household name these days outside of Macon, but in the almost lost literary years between the end of the Civil War and the beginning of this century, he wrote fiction, stories and novels, won some prizes, and wrote one book, a novella called *Aeneas Africanus*, which sold a couple of million copies over the years and, I believe, is still in print.

One of the prizes he won, before the turn of the century, was a $10,000 national award for the novel *Sons and Fathers* (which I have to admit I haven't read). Ten thousand dollars! That was a lot of money in those days. All I know is what he did with it. He rented a whole railroad car, a Pullman, and took his family and friends to New York City and back. While in New York City they managed to spend all of it. This infuriated my grandfather, to whom, evidently, Edwards owed some money. But the story of it delighted me. That's what being a writer was all about.

On the other side of the family there was a handsome and glamorous uncle who seemed to confirm that truth. A highly decorated hero of the First World War, a star reporter and feature writer in New York, he was lured to Hollywood when talking pictures came in and he had thirty years of a busy and successful career as a screenwriter. What that meant to me—I was his godson—was fabulous expensive presents at Christmastime and birthdays. And once in a great while he would appear suddenly (always briefly) at the wheel of incredible automobiles, all of them with superchargers and spoked wheels as I remember them, unlike any ever seen in the state of Florida. In the car there was always a beautiful, mysterious woman. Also unlike any that I had ever seen. His wives, interchangeable in the perfection of face and form. He would appear without warning in our lives, a sudden bright flare like a struck match in a dark room. Then he would vanish, going about his own mysterious business. That was being a writer. . . .

What being a writer was *not* about was exemplified by my kind and generous Aunt Helen Garrett. Who wrote some of the finest children's books I have ever read, before or since. Wonderful books, every one of them. The only thing was that what she really wanted to be was a novelist. And, as I heard early, she had written and was constantly working on and revising a semi-autobiographical novel of the years she had spent as a nurse in a remote part of Newfoundland. Nobody wanted it. They wanted her children's books and they would publish anything she wrote for children. But not a novel about a hard life in Newfoundland. Family wisdom was that there was something seriously wrong with her thinking. Why devote yourself to doing something that nobody wanted?

Not that I wasn't aware of failure as a part of the writing life. My uncle the screenwriter wrote a Broadway play in the 1930s, a wonderful play about Hitler, whom he had met and interviewed more than once, beginning in 1923, and whom he took to be a very dangerous person. The play opened a couple of days after the Munich Pact of 1938. The critics said it was a wonderful play, exciting and adventurous in form, powerful. Only, they added, Hitler was now no longer a threat to Western civilization or anybody else. He was now irrelevant and, well, just a little boring. The play closed after a few performances and Americans went merrily along daydreaming. A year or so later and people like Orson Welles and Robert E. Sherwood and Maxwell Anderson, with more recent events to inspire them, discovered there was gold in them-there Fascist Hills.

What was the lesson to learn? Timing. That timing was almost everything. And luck—pure, dumb luck.

In school and college I began to discover writers and writing. The honored dead, of course, as Dylan Thomas put it, "with their nightingales and psalms." And the moderns—Hemingway, Fitzgerald, Faulkner, all three represented in the Viking Portable Library editions.

Being a writer then became going to war and living to tell the tale, going on safari and shooting lions and other big animals, skinny-dipping in the fountain in front of the Plaza Hotel, and living in a crumbling cobwebby old Southern mansion. And I could see real writers up close and personal on the junior faculty at my university—Jarrell and Schwartz and Berryman and Bellow; and, younger than they, but already wonderfully successful, Frederick Buechner, author of *A Long Day's Dying*. (Remember that one?) You could see him at the Princeton junction station, trench coat and attaché case, waiting for the train to New York City and probably planning to enjoy a multi-martini lunch with his publisher. That was being a writer.

About that time, my grandfather, then in his nineties, asked me what I planned to do with myself in real life when I grew up. I allowed as how I intended to be a writer. I am grateful that, in the end, I received his blessing. First, though, he wanted to know what in the world I would ever find to write about. Nothing, he assured me, of much interest had yet happened to me or was likely to. I hadn't done anything. Maybe I couldn't do anything.

I had no good answer to that. Something would come to me, I opined.

There followed then a thoughtful pause, a silence. I expected the worst, not giving myself a moment to imagine the world from his point of view. He had five sons—one with regular and reliable employment as a cavalry officer as long as the U.S. Army continued to have horse cavalry; one was a musician and one a dancer; one was a professional golfer; and one whose great talent was the game of baseball, but who was not presently exercising that talent, being confined in what (in that era) was politely called an insane asylum. It didn't occur to me that, from my grandfather's standpoint, a writer in the family might actually be an *improvement* in social status. Nor did it occur to me then and there that all I had to do was to tell him, in answer to his skepticism of my ability to find subject matter, that I had the family, his family, to write about.

A long, thoughtful pause, and then he passed judgment: "Well, that's all right," he said. "Being a writer is as good a way to be poor as any other." He was right about that, anyway, though he didn't live to see the living proof of it.

A little later, coming out of a couple of years overseas with the Army, I found myself in graduate school on the GI Bill, plus a modest little fellowship that nobody else seemed to want. I was married and studying English, though really just biding and passing the time. Very soon, I told myself and my wife and anybody else who would listen without laughing, I would write something wonderful. And then I would be a rich and famous writer. Meanwhile, however, it was nice to have the prospect of a day job ahead—just in case I needed it. Not a job as a writer. Very few schools, next to none, hired writers in those days. Unforeseeably, unimaginably, within a few years all that would change—radically. As I move steadily toward my retirement from the academy—that, by the way, shows how well my casual life plan worked out; I'm still waiting to be a rich and famous writer—nowadays there are hundreds of writers of all ages and at all stages working in the groves of academe. In fact, at this instant, the overwhelming majority of living American writers are college educated. And most of them, for better and worse, now work in and for colleges and universities.

Some of you, maybe all of you, can think of exceptions to that generalization. So can I . . . but, I'm sad to report, even the most independent spirits are, one way or another, however indirectly, connected with the academy. Nobody has the slightest idea what this condition is going to do and to mean to American literature. One thing that it has done, a positive thing on the whole, is to make it possible for all kinds of groups and minorities to have some kind of a public literary voice. To report their version of events. To tell their own stories, true and false.

Another thing that is happening, a negative thing on the whole, is the multiple forces of subtle and sometimes not so subtle pressure for the employee-writer to become and be an institutional person, a happy camper within the institution, successful within the institution, bringing visibility and credit to the institution, and, yes sirree, thinking and acting correctly within the socio-political context of the institution.

One thing, among many, that this has meant is that the writer in the institution will not, does not, seriously consider dealing with intractable and controversial subjects. Since most of the important matters in the real world at the tag end of our sorry century are controversial and often intractable, the writer has to go to great lengths to try to find something else to write about. My grandfather's question applies now more than ever.

More and more American literary art isn't about anything that matters to anybody. In the larger society, beginning in the educational institutions to be sure, the writer also has to come to terms with the culture of celebrity. That's a huge problem, a black cloud that follows all of us around.

When image is everything, what is fiction and where does it come into our lives? Or, in a more practical sense, when celebrity—that is, identification, public recognition of any kind—is what matters, the writer is sorely tempted to strive to create a brand name, to find something that works and to repeat it endlessly, mindlessly. And likewise the writer who has achieved a modicum of celebrity will not, as a rule, risk that capital by too-frequent tests and trials in the public arena. It's as if you could preserve your batting average by not coming to the plate too much.

Which is all well and good if what we are interested in is a well-mapped literary scene, a consensual hierarchy that is to the advantage, the vested interest of writers, critics, and scholars and, of course, the institutions that own all of them, to preserve and maintain.

But if it is art you are thinking about, hoping for, there must be constant risk-taking and productivity, there must be (inevitably) ups and downs. To do good things, worthy work, artists must risk failure, must, indeed, fail from time to time. The Roman poet Martial put it very clearly and simply a couple of thousand years ago:

> To my reader: When you look
> inside, you're bound to find here
> some good verses, some middling, and I fear
> plenty of bad ones. What can I say:
> Buddy, it's the only way a poet can make a book.

One other inhibiting factor in the culture of celebrity, seldom mentioned or seriously discussed, is the decline of New York from national city to shrinking region, a place characterized by all the defensiveness and vulnerability that has haunted other regional societies. Unfortunately for the rest of us all, though particularly writers scattered across this wide huge country, New York remains the center of publishing and of associated publicity. Which means that work created elsewhere must first and foremost pass muster with the regional powers-that-be in New York. Because of *our* modesty and passivity, we are perfectly willing to accept that situation. Let them pass judgment. Let them rate and rank things. It saves us a lot of trouble and effort, and it spares us from the embarrassment of making mistakes on our own.

Unfortunately, contemporary publishing in New York is run by people who are weirdly compounded. They are as *ignorant* as anyone else. But, at one and the same time, they are jaded, sophisticated, bored, silly. They are looking for palliatives for *that* condition. They have neither any idea nor interest in what *we* might care about or be concerned with. There is an abyss between us.

It is hard to imagine that the situation of the stubby tail wagging the very large dog can go on forever. And it probably won't. But while it lasts, we have to live and work with it. Unless and until we are prepared to declare our intellectual independence.

Time will tell about that.

And time will tell if the writing life was wise or foolish, happy or sad. Certainly it has been and remains interesting. My bumper sticker, albeit attached to the bumper of a beat-up old car, a happy heap, reads: "No Regrets." I can live with that, coming or going.

Meanwhile what becomes of a writer is an abstraction a résumé, sometimes including a selected bibliog raphy. Neither tells the whole truth. My résumé offers all kinds of facts, though only some of the facts, and even then is only as accurate as memory and goodwill can make it. With all of its absences and ellipses, its strict limitations, it remains no more than a kind of shadowy source. And a bibliography lists books in the order of their publication and, of course, can tell or suggest nothing at all about their composition, transformation, publication, reception, etc. Some things came easily and quickly. *Which Ones Are the Enemy?* took three full weeks to write. *Death of the Fox* and *Poison Pen* and *The King of Babylon Shall Not Come Against You* were twenty-year labors. Some things on the list started out to be something quite different than what they became. For example, the novel *Do, Lord, Remember Me* was, in its finished versions, twice as long as it is now, and I still think of it as half of a book. I used the plural ("its finished versions") because there were two distinctly different versions published, one in England, the other in America. I am not sure to this day which of the two is better; though, for various reasons, I favor the British version. And it is that text that the L.S.U. Press published in their "Voices of the South" series.

Reception? Whimsically different. Some were prominently noticed and well-received, and some were not. A glance at the history of these books would lead at once to the conclusion that it has all been hit or miss. Though I cannot claim that any kind of review or notice has helped me as a writer (I know the flaws and weaknesses of my work better than anyone else can), I am always grateful for any favorable review. What does any of it mean? Once upon a time, when I was young (and foolish), it all seemed to matter a great deal. Sometimes when I couldn't sleep, I tried to put myself to sleep not by counting sheep, but by calling up innumerable rejections, slights, insults, put-downs, bad reviews, and bad times. But it turned out there were too many of all of these things to remember. I had forgotten half of them. It had always been my uncomfortable intention to forget and forgive. But I was forgetting before I had a chance to forgive. All of my wounds seemed to have come from pratfalls.

All but a few—and how I cherish the precious few!—have paid next to no attention to my work during the forty and more years since I first began to publish it. But every other artist and writer, even the most celebrated, has to experience and admit the same thing. There are no numbers. All but the precious few are false. So there are only the precious few. And they are an unearned blessing. The living ones know who they are. Among the dead, who are now beyond praise or blame, I am profoundly grateful, beyond all measuring and telling, to a host of kinfolk, to certain school teachers and coaches and trainers, even to certain superiors and commanding officers. And there are writers, long gone now, to whom I owe much. I am especially grateful for the good interest and loving kindness, for encouragement and companionship, to Marianne Moore and Babette Deutsch, John Ciardi and John Hall Wheelock, James Dickey and Jesse Hill Ford, R.P. Blackmur and Rolfe Humphries, William Goyen and Roger Rath and Paxton Davis.

Years ago, Shelby Foote came to the University of Virginia for a week-long residency. One day he visited my creative writing class. He talked a while, then invited questions. Aware that he had known William Faulkner, one of the students asked him what Faulkner was really like.

"Have you read the books?" Foote asked.

"Yes, sir."

Well, then, Foote answered, that was it. That is all there is. Nothing more and nothing less. William Faulkner became what he always wanted to be—his work.

And there it was, a precise and articulate formulation of exactly what I had hoped for, dreamed of, without knowing it. Ever since then, the shape of that idea, the perfection and the purity of it, has haunted me. Let my whole life be only in my work and everywhere equally, whether in a long, knotty novel or the verse lines of a brisk epigram.

Now at an age I never imagined reaching, it has at last come home to me that the ideal is fallacious, that there is no way to disappear forever into the work. Not for Faulkner, not for me or anyone. I have lived a good long time since that day in class and have learned and changed a little. One of the things I have learned is that whether I wanted it to be so or not, the plain facts of my life, the *facts* and not merely the ghostly shadows of them, are at the heart of all my work. I alone (I hope) could recognize these things in their motley disguises. But they are there, nevertheless. No denying it. In truth, I move along as naked as the fairy-tale emperor in his brand new clothes, in everything I have ever written (including this piece). My chief pride and joy being that everything I have written, be it ever so humble and slight, light-hearted or frivolous, graceful or inept, contains (more or less) the same truth of myself. And to that extent I may have succeeded. If only by turning Shelby Foote's proposition inside out.

How the Cookie Crumbled:
Notes on a Literary Generation

We, the writers who came of age and on the literary scene (visibly or invisibly) in the years immediately following World War II, are a genuine generation: I am thinking not of the convenient measurement used (and abused) by literary journalists—the decade. Rather I am thinking of the old-fashioned idea of a generation, a full quarter century, and not neat, with overlapping at both ends. Almost all of us served in the armed forces during World War II and/or the Korean War. Most of us came to grown-up consciousness then, shadowed by a constant awareness of the atomic bomb and the ever-growing worldwide nuclear arsenal. Many of us, on the basis of experience and the evidence at hand, did not even imagine, let alone believe, that we would live as long as we have without a major nuclear war. In our twenties and thirties, many of us doubted we would live into our forties and fifties. This became an unspoken factor in our lives significant enough to have merited mention and consideration by William Faulkner in his 1950 Nobel Prize address, which was, in large part, directed to the next generation of writers. He was talking to us. He saw through the bravado and shrugging cynicism affected by a lot of us. He identified the unseemly core of our attitude—fear, pure and simple. That fear, at least at the outset, helped to define us and to shape the form and content of our work.

Another factor that helped to define us and the work we have done or left undone is the particular literary scene in which we have been cast and played out our parts, major or minor. An important corollary to this generalization is that very few, if any, of us realized that our generation was marked by significant differences from the previous generation—that amazing generation of the great modern masters: Joyce, Proust, and Mann; Hemingway, Fitzgerald, and Faulkner; Pound and Eliot. We simply imagined ourselves to be younger and maybe less-gifted versions of these people, living in roughly the same world and working under roughly the same conditions, able, therefore, to profit directly by and from their examples and, indeed, able to learn many practical things from them. This same misperception allowed us the illusion that given time and some occasion (and a little bit of luck), there could be some justice in the literary world. For example: Fitzgerald was "rediscovered" and restored to reputation in the years right after the war; and, for all but a few, Faulkner was found and honored for the first time. The comfort of that illusion—that justice and recognition were possible in the long run—played directly against our certainty that we would all be blown to atoms and sky-high any day of the year.

Years of hard experience have taught me that we were wrong about all this; in truth, we live in a radically different world from that of the earlier generation of modern masters. I have also very gradually become aware that they, too, the masters, misapprehended their own literary scene and situation, not unreasonably believing themselves to be merely younger and bolder versions of the late-nineteenth-century and early-twentieth-century masters. Even as the modernists were in open rebellion against the ways and means of that earlier generation, they seem to have believed that, in fact, they shared the same turf and were fighting to possess it.

In any case, I conclude that by and large and for several generations, writers, at least American writers, have done their work with an uncertain, often illusory concept of their own literary situation. And I notice that this continues. For our youngest writers, the final generation of this century, seem to believe that they inhabit the same world that we, their elders, do. But the inescapable truth is that the literary world has changed sharply and significantly since the days when we were young and beginning.

Which leads me to my topic: how it really was for us, how things were and are constantly changing, for good and for ill, all around us. You can start the investigation almost anywhere. With formal education, for example. I have plenty of anecdotal evidence and every good reason to doubt that many of my own generation were or are as deeply and well read as most of our elders. Yet we had more formal education. Fitzgerald never finished at Princeton, while we ended up, the overwhelming majority of us, going to college. The GI Bill did it for us. Suddenly, a complete college education, such as it was, was not beyond the expectations or the means of many more Americans than ever before. Just so, a college degree soon became a necessity, the basic ticket for all kinds of jobs that had not until then required a high school diploma. Our generation went to school a lot longer than most of the writers of the earlier generation. Pretty soon, a radical new wrinkle at the time, we found ourselves actually studying the literary works of the twentieth-century masters. For better or worse, they (or some of them, anyway) became "required reading." Shortly afterwards, if not simultaneously, the teaching of the art and craft of creative writing, something that had previously been underground or disguised, began to be part of the conventional curriculum of the first-rate colleges and universities. Within a brief time, brief enough as these things go, creative writing became a part of the curriculum of almost all American colleges and universities. As this began to happen, the institutions soon needed writers to teach these courses, and they hired them to do so. Thus the writers—poets as much as fiction writers—moved into the ambiguous shade of the groves of academe. Whereas the earlier generation had depended on newspapers and Hollywood or, maybe, a position in the professions or, anyway, rich spouses, for survival and to support the writing habit; and where hard times and the code of the class system had made it almost impossible for many people seriously to consider following the writer's life and trade, all that changed when the academies became the principal patrons for "serious" contemporary literature.

One of the (perhaps) positive results of this alliance between the academies and literary artists was that it helped to make it possible for new voices, from widely diverse classes and ethnic groups and tribes, to be heard. And with writers settling in everywhere as full-fledged, lifetime faculty members, it was inevitable that the patron institutions would judge and reward (or punish) the productivity and "visibility" of these employees. Reviews, grants and fellowships, prizes and honors paid off directly in cash or promotions, conditions not likely to encourage radical challenging or risk-taking artistic adventures but at least calling for a high degree of recognizable competence. It was also now completely plausible for the university presses to begin to publish more poetry and fiction than ever before, an expanding trend that has continued from the late 1950s to the present. At first, publication by a university press was looked upon by the writers themselves as somehow inferior, *déclassé*. It was better and conferred more status to be published by one of the major commercial publishers. I remember that when I had a chance to publish my second book of poems, *The Sleeping Gypsy* (1958), under very favorable conditions, including a surprising (for the time) $2,500 advance, with the University of Texas Press, I was strongly advised by writers whom I knew and admired and took to be good friends not to do this but patiently to wait my turn and place with the major New York publishers. At just about the same time, Wesleyan University, where I was working as a teacher, was beginning to crank up what was to become the Wesleyan Poetry Series. One of the things worrying the Wesleyan University Press at the time was how they would ever manage to attract the attention and interest of gifted, important poets. Within a very short time they found themselves swamped with submitted manuscripts, able to pick and choose as they pleased.

Nowadays it is simply a fact that university presses and small presses are major players in the publication of poetry and "serious" (now called "literary") fiction, a fact that remains amazing to those of us who witnessed the beginning of the trend. Over those years I (typically, I think) published books with commercial American publishers such as Scribners; Little, Brown; Doubleday; Morrow; Norton; Harcourt Brace; and also with a string of university presses: North Carolina, Missouri, Arkansas, South Carolina, Southern Methodist, Wesleyan, Virginia.

(In passing, I should note that this variety of publishers for any one writer is more or less typical of my generation, and not at all the case with the earlier generation. Only a very few of us, John Updike, for example, have been with the same house all along.)

Not all the results of the association of writers and the universities have been positively worthwhile. As indicated earlier, in return for support the academies hope for the highest possible visibility for their employee-writers. This goal, manifestly rewarded with raises, promotion, and tenure (and more free time for writing), puts real pressure on the writers to be highly productive, to publish, and to do so often or to perish, to earn favorable notice of published work and, as much as may be possible, to bring notice and distinction to the patron institution. At the least, one must allow that these general, institutional goals have tended to emphasize values other than artistic quality. Even without the deconstructive theorists' doubts that literary quality exists, quality has increasingly become whatever is consensually recognized and reported as being such. That is, then, a distinctly different goal from that of the earlier generation. One must likewise admit that the dependency upon academic institutional support has created a danger that bold and original work, like that of the modernist masters, work cutting against the grain of present theory and current critical fashions, will be strictly inhibited. Once the writers accepted and adapted to the terms of academic patronage, as the overwhelming majority have, in fact, done, it is only a hop, skip, and jump to accepting and adapting to the prevailing winds, the climate of institutional opinion. For example, one of the widely recognized results of the tumultuous 1960s was the assembly, first as students, then as faculty, of large numbers of people who originally sought safety and sanctuary from the rigors and dangers of military service and later (now) looked for a safe haven for various forms and kinds of leftist political positions, some of which are already emphatically discredited in the wider ("real") world. The problems and serious dangers of being found out as not "politically correct" in the context of the contemporary academic milieu have been widely discussed and debated elsewhere. What has not yet been articulated is how this peculiar cultural condition can and, it seems to me, has affected American writing. For the writer in the university to conform and to endure, there are not only matters of opinion that are either unquestioned or forbidden (taboo), but also there are whole areas of subject matter, *subjects* that can only be treated gingerly, very carefully, if at all. One of the major and legitimate complaints against contemporary American literary fiction—and this applies to poetry as well—is how it has more and more come to avoid dealing with the serious daily problems, the "real" problems of the real world. Or, if and when writers treat serious contemporary concerns, how they do so from an extremely limited and reflexive (thoughtless) point of view.

There is a great irony here—that, at the outset, when writers of my generation were first being welcomed into the academies, it seemed to be the hope and expectation of the traditional academics that the writers would bring new blood and spirit into the academic world; and, indeed, in the early days, the writers were encouraged and expected to be colorful rebels, an expectation that has, in a short time, been greatly modified.

Meantime, the publishing business, the other vital institution for writers, has changed beyond simple description or believing during the same generation. It is not merely a matter of mergers and the consequent growth of common corporate practices and attitudes, though; in fact, these attitudes and practices have next to nothing to do with the earlier concepts and models of what publishing ought to be. It is also the discovery and acceptance of the truth that mediocre, even blatantly bad books can be marketed as "blockbusters" and can sometimes earn huge profits for everyone concerned. Couple this practice with another peculiarly contemporary symptom, the absence of any personal or social shame in the society at large, so that a publisher of *schlock* need not be, as earlier publishers certainly were or feared to be, embarrassed or in any way seriously injured by sleazy publishing habits, and we are faced with a literary situation not conducive to the development of literary quality.

Then there is the matter of relentless change, exploding technology—the whole new world of the computer, the Internet, e-mail, cyberspace, electronic publishing. Clearly these things and others will change everything else in mostly unforeseen and unimaginable ways. Some of them may prove to be positive, possibly improvements, as was the printing press. And it demonstrates neither special courage nor excessive confidence to assert that because we have had writers even before we had writing or anything to write on or with, we will continue to need storytellers and tales of joy and woe in the new world.

Every writer I know of is fully aware of all these things. At the least, that knowledge tends to make writers deeply cynical and, all too often, at the same time desperately competitive. In American poetry and literary fiction there are stars. But they have an appointed rather than an earned status because, for the most part, in the marketplace they sell about the same number of copies as their lesser known and even unknown peers. This kind of uneasy, unearned status has tended to make its lucky beneficiaries extremely defensive of the status quo. It, too, tends to inhibit any urge toward originality. It is difficult to imagine any American writer of my generation (except maybe a bona fide hermit) creating something of such powerful originality as *The Sound and the Fury* or *The Great Gatsby* or *The Wasteland*. There are just too many disincentives.

Many of us in my generation now can see that we were not moving on the same track as the earlier generation, that we have been fighting losing battles and rearguard actions the whole time, even when we thought we were advancing on all fronts. Part of our source of error lay in the belief that our lives and work would be much like that of the admirable generation before ours. Meantime, at our backs we have been hearing the horns and hounds of yet another generation, a new one, assured of certain certainties as much as we were and, for the time being, undaunted, not likely to believe anything I have said here and unlikely to be dismayed or deterred in any case. All of which is, after all, just as well. Folly it may prove to be, but without that foolishness we would have to settle for all that is left—the bitter silence of the undeceived.

Cowboys and Indians: A Few Notions about Creative Writing

This little piece requires a head note. Oddly, it is the only thing I have ever written that was honest-to-God censored. I was asked by *The Chronicle of Higher Education* to write a short opinion piece on the subject of contemporary creative writing courses etc.—the scene. I wrote this piece, following their guidelines exactly for length and general tone. After a while it came back to me with the explanation that they didn't approve of my opinions. Not at all. They didn't even suggest *revising* my opinions. Beyond the pale. See if you can figure out why. I can't.

In the beginning we were the rebels. The real beginning was during the late forties and early fifties, that astonishing time on the GI Bill when American colleges and universities were suddenly booming and changing. We asked for courses in twentieth-century literature, and we got that, together with fair and accurate warning from the elders that the canon would, sooner or later, constitute a bloody battlefield. Along with that we wanted the opportunity to write our poems and stories and novels on the institution's time and for credit. Won that one, too, and so completely that now there are poets and writers teaching writing courses in hundreds of colleges and universities. It was been a radical change far beyond the wildest expectations of the very few of us, raggedy in our faded fatigues and field jackets, who came out of the jungle and mountains to civilization. Our fearless leader (Fidel) was (is) R. V. Cassill, first at Iowa, then Brown. We were few in number as late as the middle sixties when Cassill and his wife, Kay, founded and managed the Associated Writing Programs (AWP) in the basement of their house in Providence. There were a dozen or so member institutions then, though there were already many schools with writers on the faculty and with courses and programs. We had so little visibility and money and clout at first that other writers and schools took a wait-and-see attitude and maintained that until, finally, AWP got some real support, big bucks. Then, led by Iowa, which had spurned joining anything with others, everybody jumped on board. Nowadays there is a headquarters with a paid bureaucracy and a newsletter and a job list and prizes and annual conventions and plenty of members eager to be elected to a list of officers. A new (ancient) crowd.

And here am I, an old-timer already, still following the leader (Cassill said it first, if differently) urging that we now take a giant step back and at least weigh and reconsider the values and dangers arising out of the association of writers with the academy. Undergraduate creative writing courses probably should continue, be kept alive and well. Close reading and closely watched writing are essential components in the lost battles against functional illiteracy. It's most of the graduate programs I wonder about, the ones that these days furnish so many books to publishers and most of the teachers of creative writing. There are superb writing programs. Hollins College is the best. And a very different kind of program at Arkansas is equally praiseworthy. Most of them, however, are depressingly uniform and uniformly mediocre. Just lately there have been some strong, cogently argued critical pieces about writing programs. Eve Shelnutt's "Notes From a Cell: Creative Writing Programs in Isolation" (*AWP Chronicle*, February 1990) and John W. Aldridge's "American Assembly-Line Fiction" (*American Scholar*, Winter 1990) make strong cases against the acquired bad habits and results of writing programs. Both are critical of the anti-intellectualism (read: *ignorance*) of the programs, the hierarchical networking (what Aldridge calls "this highly politicized fraternity of writing instruction"); and both are seriously concerned by the absence of normative models and of eclectic diversity in the programs and their products and, also, by the changing relationship of the writer and society.

These points are well taken, but I have others, based on years of experience in the trenches as an employee of several different kinds of institutions. Seems to me that our colleges and universities—I speak almost exclusively of the vague humanities, sparing science, engineering etc., where, even in the most theoretical of modes, there is less tinkering with and distortion of hard facts—are a mirror image of the world and the times they inhabit. The institutions are not nearly as separate from the common vices and virtues of the age as they often imagine themselves to be; though both vices and virtues are often camouflaged by a certain respectability, which Americans, innocently enough, still attribute to educators and educational institutions. Thus, I have to argue that there are probably no more liars, thieves, cheaters, polluters (real and metaphorical), criminals, and invincibly ignorant incompetents within the institutions than there are in society at large. But no fewer either.

Once upon a time in Los Angeles, I found myself at lunch with a group of talent agents, sharks of the movie industry, where conversation was all about the insatiable appetites of the great white sharks at the top of the Hollywood food chain. Eager to join in, I told them a couple of anecdotes about feeding frenzy in academe. Shocked them thoroughly. Left them open-mouthed. "Do you mean people like that are allowed to teach our children?" they asked.

Our contemporary institutions of higher learning are built on the corporate model without benefit of the checks and balances that are required to produce a worthwhile product and to turn a profit. To the pervasive administrative inefficiency and complacency and incompetence that has always plagued us must be added a full share of the other woes and faults and tribulations of the age. We have more than enough of our own Boeskys and Trumps and Milkens. And some of them are poets and fiction writers who know no other world or way of life. One good reason for writers to dissociate themselves from academe is to avoid the bad company there, including the bad company of each other.

But there are some better reasons. One of these is the chilling effect on freedom of speech and thought that is felt, not only aesthetically but also politically and socially by writers in an academic context these days. Since amiable visibility and consequent prizes and honors are urgently important to the artist in academe, there is a serious disincentive to any experimentation beyond the most commonplace gimmickry and any exploitation of unfashionable notions that might seem to challenge the *beaux arts* establishment. Originality is defined as finding your place and staying in it. On an aesthetic level this deprives us all of variety (choices). On a political and social level, with the brown- and black-shirt children of the sixties now safely arrived at middle age and position in academe, there is a tendency toward an unquestioning, reflexive uniformity of thought and language, which limits intellectual inquiry and discourages the kind of critical scrutiny out of which true innovation may come to pass. If "correct" political and social stances are required for promotion and tenure (and they certainly are), the artist will either conform or, anyway, limit himself/herself to the aesthetic level of experience.

Is it any wonder that we have just finished a decade of some of the most polished and boring poetry and some of the most competent and inconsequential fiction in our national history? If the situation were not so dangerous, it would be simply farcical.

Easy and safe to say for one so near to retirement age anyway, but nevertheless I am convinced that we have now outgrown the good (and there was some) of the close association of writers and academe. Writers would be better off in almost any other line of work. An exception is those underclass and minority writers whose voices, previously unheard, would be lost to us again without some special support. And, of course, such a course would be hard on the poets, many of whom lack even basic entry-level skills; but perhaps this could be corrected by programs in vocational training.

Yesterday's rebels are today's fat cats, and the last great concentration of unreconstructed Marxists (not counting Albania) is now to be found in our English departments. My view is simply that writers, young and old, will be well advised to slip out of the circle of wagons and rejoin the lively Indians riding on the outside.

Preface to "Lives of the Poets"

Light and steady a falling rain
on the York River and now my ghosts,
friends and enemies, arrive again
to look over my bent shoulders
even as I am writing these words
on a yellow pad, on a zinc worktable.
I met some poets, knew some others
better who didn't know me from Adam
and Eve; and therefore I could watch
them sometimes at very close range
and not be noticed. Myself in uniform,
U.S. Army, noticed and yet anonymous,
among the very few who came to listen to
Homage to Mistress Bradstreet's first
public outing, long before Henry
and much more a matter of Keats's
"fine excess" than any jazz and jive.
Thinking even then as I listened
to that knotty syntax, those lovely words,
how once I stood in line directly
behind Berryman in a liquor store
on Nassau Street after a football game.
Clerk to Berryman: "May I help?"
Berryman: "I want to buy a bottle."
"Very good. Bottle of what, sir?"
"I am a poet, my good man.

Don't trouble me with petty details
and distinctions." Clerk nodded politely
and found and climbed a rickety ladder
to the highest shelf from which
he freed a dusty quart of Ouzo,
blew a cloud of that dust away
and, poker-faced, presented it
to the poet as if it were a chalice.
Poet paid and staggered outside
into a softly dimming twilight,
holding his prize like a new baby.
Left me to picture him in the dark
kneeling somewhere, lawn or toilet bowl,
barfing his licorice heart out.
They spoiled you at Princeton, John,
as they have done some others, lucky and not,
including most recently the sly Muldoon.
Randall Jarrell did not feel so honored,
said and wrote (remember?) he felt
like a prize pig wandering around
the county fair. The judges saying
"Go away, pig! What do you know
about bacon?" In Greensboro, NC
Jarrell walked right out of my reading
pleading that it was much too hot
to sit there and listen. He was right,
but I was very young, too young
even to be much wounded until now.
But back then, before that time,
at Princeton these were all there—
Berryman, Jarrell, Bellow, Delmore Schwartz,
who, young and foolish as they really were,
seemed older and even more foolish to us,
young and impatient as we surely were.

Merwin and Meredith, Holmes and Cox,
Bink Noll and Kinnell, we were too busy
scorning each other to more than ignore
them one and all. Peace Richard Blackmur,
you were the kindly father to us all.
Peace also to that good man, Tom Riggs,
who may of them all then living have been
the best and most gifted, but died young.
Dylan Thomas came there twice and once
at the Nassau Tavern at a round table
of at least a dozen poets, all ages
and stages, dared them to make a limerick
ending with "Edna St. Vincent Millay."
Nobody among them succeeded on that
occasion, and I remember witnessing
that dozen prominent poets in a row
at the urinals in the Men's Room
when the burly bartender banged
on the door and loudly announced:
"Hurry up, please, it's time!"
A dozen gold streams cut off instantly.
T. S. Eliot, tall as a crane and black
as a crow, found a seat by a student
(me) to listen to a lecture.
On my other side sat Jacques Maritain,
whose star was burning bright.
Student sat still, said nothing,
made not a sound, of breath, belch or fart. . . .

Steady now, the rain is needling
the high tide and the seagulls huddle
wherever they can and keep quiet.
Ghost me, then, gulls and angels
and you dead poets, some of whom,

named in due time, as good or better
than any of these and all of them
near as my left shoulder and as far
away as that lost youth when words
burned like neon, candles, torches,
searchlights flashing across triumphant dark,
the dark which takes the poets, one and all,
into its arms, holds us like Ouzo or hurt children
and gently awards the democratic prizes
of perfect silence, of honorable oblivion.

Other Voices

The Good Ghost of F. Scott Fitzgerald: A Talk to the Fitzgerald Society

It is easy to forget that not all that long ago, at least measured in the spent years of my own lifetime, this gathering would have been almost unimaginable. Not that each and every serious and gifted writer (and even some not so serious or so gifted) is not perfectly capable of imagining a future so blessed with some vaguely similar honor—a gathering of friends and scholars and critics to celebrate the writer's work and name. Certainly Fitzgerald had every reason to hope, perhaps at the sad end to pray, too, that his life's work had earned something more than the genteel oblivion of the darkest and dustiest inches of library stacks. In his finest and happiest hours, perhaps more than most of his peers, he may well have been able to imagine that more than a half-century after his death, there would be people who would love and support his art and would stand up for it in new and different and, in many ways, unimaginable times. Fitzgerald was more acutely aware of his own times—the details, the flowering and the withering of the present— than most of our writers. He was more sensitive to change and decay than most, and for precisely that reason he would be (according to my guess) more startled and maybe delighted by the idea of a gathering of academics in his honor and, maybe just as much so, by the presence of a living and working writer (myself) in the same company.

And so would I be surprised if I had not lived in and through the half century since his death and been witness to and participant in much of the changing.

It is that changing that is my chief subject. I want to deal with it in a form that is odd enough to be misunderstood, though I hope that it will not be. Although I am speaking openly enough about myself, my true and proper subject is the powerful and continuing, though always changing, influence of the life and art of Scott Fitzgerald on American literature. I call myself to the witness stand not, by any means, claiming any special value or importance to myself as witness or to my work, but because the example and influence of Fitzgerald has been strong, continuous, and constantly changing. In that sense I can claim to be typical of a great many American writers—poets as well as fiction writers—of roughly my age and generation and of the younger generation, too, coming on strongly as our century, this bloody and brutal century, staggers toward its bitter end.

Summer of 1948, a green, cool, pleasant summer in Princeton, New Jersey. It was the last summer school held at Princeton University, at least from then until now. Princeton, where the student body was still predominately made up of veterans home from World War II, eager to finish up their formal education and to resume their real lives. It was the first time that the Princeton English Department offered a course in British and American literature published after 1900. This was English 251, for the record, and to the best of my recollection, taught by a young assistant professor named John Hite. The lectures took place in one of the big rooms, McCosh 10 or McCosh 30, I think, an eight o'clock class and always jam-packed. We read *The Wasteland* and *The Sun Also Rises* and *The Sound and the*

Fury and, for F. Scott Fitzgerald, here being officially taught for the first time at his own school, we had *The Portable F. Scott Fitzgerald*. *Gatsby* was assigned for the course, together with some parts of *The Crack-Up*, which was on reserve at the brand new Firestone Library. As late as that summer, first editions of Fitzgerald's books rested quietly and openly on the open stacks of the Library. So did Faulkner's first editions at that same time. Not for long, to be sure. It is also a fact that as late as that same summer, almost halfway through our century, very, very few colleges yet offered any courses at all in twentieth-century literature.

And so it was more than discovery; it was vaguely illicit to be reading writers more or less of the same age as our parents and some of them still much alive and writing. I had already read a lot of Hemingway. I had heard a little (from other readers in the family) about William Faulkner.

But Fitzgerald was entirely new to me; though, for various reasons, I should have had a little knowledge and more interest. Also at that time there were very few American writers working at colleges and universities. There was always Frost, a regular visitor at Amherst; and there were a few others scattered here and there at one place and another, including Iowa, which was cranking up under the direction of Paul Engle. But the established connection between living and working writers and the Academy had not quite come to pass. It had never been a serious or valuable possibility for Fitzgerald's generation. When writers were brought into the groves of academe at all, they slipped in the back door and maintained a low profile. Thanks to Allen Tate and to R. P. Blackmur we had at Princeton several young writers acting as instructors—Randall Jarrell, John Berryman, Delmore Schwartz, and Saul Bellow among others. My preceptor in English 251 was the poet (and legitimate Ph.D.) Louis Coxe. But it was still a few years into the future before Dylan Thomas would show up, an hour or so late, to be sure, and entertain an enthusiastic audience in McCosh 30.

We were assigned *The Great Gatsby*, and we read some pages of *The Crack-Up;* and since the Viking Portable edition also had stories and the whole of *Tender Is the Night*, we read and talked about those, too, though not as an assignment.

And where was I in those days? Well, Hemingway was writing about exciting and, it seemed, relevant things; and he had that style, more aptly and recently called, by Elmore Leonard, that "attitude." Faulkner was wild and woolly, throwing around great gobs of words the way, some years later, Jackson Pollack would be splashing paint. His subjects and places and people were familiar, down-home, close enough to be part of my own experience.

Fitzgerald seemed more of a straight arrow than the other two, at least in the writing. He was a college boy, too, an old-fashioned "Princeton Charley." I loved all that I read, especially *Tender Is the Night*. Even as a young man, a green kid, I could admire *Gatsby*. But I loved *Tender Is the Night*. How could I not love it, when it took me directly to the Riviera, to the "bright tan prayer rug of a beach," and in less than a page was showing me a sun-glittering and wholly glamorous world as witnessed by Rosemary "who had magic in her pink palms and her cheeks lit to a lovely flame, like the thrilling flush of children after their cold baths in the evening"? Cowley's later revised edition aside, this is the only place and the only way to begin that particular story. It is illuminated by youthful witnessing and means so much more that way. It is so much more credible and moving because of the unforgettable impact of its powerful first impressions. It was only much later that I would come to recognize and to understand the technical skill of the author and the extraordinary capacity he possessed for evoking honestly and exactly the world of youth—of adolescence. It is something not at all easy to do without stumbling or pratfalls.

I loved *Tender Is the Night* and I admired *Gatsby*, and I carried the Viking Portable with me as I went to Texas, where I worked for a geophysical exploration crew; and into the Army to the Free Territory of Trieste, where I served for a time on the volatile, sometimes dangerous Yugoslav border, and then on up to Linz where an understrength regiment of us faced 40,000 of Stalin's finest on the other side of the Danube; and where our tactical mission was to try to delay them for a short period of time, somewhere between fifteen minutes and a half hour, if and when they elected to come across the river, something I have just now lately learned was entirely possible at that time.

If I carried the *Portable Fitzgerald* with me everywhere I went, I nevertheless had ambivalent, even contradictory feelings about the author, about whom, of course, I knew next to nothing except the kind of glorified gossip that only a serious and patient scholarship can and did eventually sweep away.

Meantime (as irony will have it), I could have done a lot better in getting to know him, to understand him better, anyway, if I had paid any attention to what was purely gossip. For it was all around me.

For example, for a couple of years, I shared first a room, later an apartment in New York City, with Bruce Hotchkiss, a nephew of Glenway Wescott; and we often spent weekends on the large, beautiful farm (now resting at the bottom of a reservoir) of the Wescott clan. Glenway Wescott knew a good deal about Fitzgerald, and in most ways his "The Moral of Scott Fitzgerald" (in *The New Republic* for February 1941 and reprinted in *The Crack-Up*) is right on the money. At the time, of course, as an aspiring writer, I identified with some of the parts about Princeton, especially Wescott's criticism of the English Department. Wescott wrote that although writers generally believed Fitzgerald "had the best narrative gift of the century," the English Department did not help him to understand that or to enjoy his gifts. He learned chiefly to be an appreciative critic of the works of others. It seemed to me that the English Department had not changed much, though it appeared to have some regard for the young poet W. S. Merwin and for Frederick Buechner and John Brooks, our official young novelists. And by then they even had some good things to say about Scott Fitzgerald.

On one hand I allowed myself to feel superior to him because I made the cut on the freshman football team and he didn't. Like so many others, I was already haunted and challenged by the ghost of him. There is a mild and bitter irony about this feeling also. I have written about it elsewhere in another context:

> Athletics occupied, at times, almost all my energy and desire. Beginning first with swimming—I learned to swim before I was two years old—and ending with college football where by the end of it I was wrapped in tape as any mummy from injuries of every kind. A David playing, without benefit of miracles, on a field of Goliaths. I ruined both knees, broke both feet, and covered my body with cloudy bruises. I recollect long afternoons spent in the steam and stink of the training

room, then hobbling back to my dormitory, fresh tape binding me here and there, reeking from the scents of a medley of salves and liniments, groaning (quietly, quietly, a fixed smile on my face, lest anyone should suspect my pain) as I passed by the tennis courts where there were crowds of young white men all in white and all of them trim and handsome and graceful, not Goliaths, not a one, but every one of them a Scott Fitzgerald. (This was, after all, Princeton.) They flaunted what I had to admit was style. I can still hear, by an exercise of grim willpower, the crisp, tingy sounds of tennis balls and good rackets meeting each other in autumnal air. Can still summon up the slow fading of late-afternoon light, the scent of wood smoke from somewhere not far; likewise the odor of leaf smoke—for they still innocently burned their leaf piles in those days. And in the midst of all this boy-man mummy who would then and there cheerfully have leapt into a burning leaf pile if he could have vanished into the thick, pale-gray smoke of it.

I did not know until many years later that Fitzgerald was short, also, small and compact. I might have liked him better at first if I had known that. Another item: directly behind our house in Orlando, Florida, lived a retired marine officer, James Bettes, and his family. It turned out that he was in the same class as Fitzgerald at Princeton and even lived in the same entryway and, together with many others, left Princeton to join the service in World War I. (For the record, Bettes, who always seemed a quiet and mild man, a gentle man, had served at one point as the commandant of the Portsmouth Naval Prison.) Bettes was not at all literary, but he thought that the Triangle shows that Fitzgerald and John Biggs and others had put together were quite wonderful.

Many years later I interviewed Judge John Biggs in Wilmington and had a fine day of it. One thing that came across clearly was another version of the honorable advice to trust the tale and not the teller. He described Fitzgerald as intellectually a kind of crank, but at the same time, as precise and prescient as any seer or shaman.

Meantime, on my mother's side of the family, there was my Aunt Dorothy, whose life and whose world, in her youth, was very much like that, in general and even in some details, of Zelda Sayre of Alabama. They were astonishingly alike, really, and though they never met, Dorothy came to know a good deal about Zelda. Dorothy was engaged to a Princeton classmate of Fitzgerald named Henry Dunn. After the war, Dunn was in New York working at the same time as Fitzgerald, whom he greatly admired, and evidently they saw a good deal of each other for a while. He wrote letters to Dorothy every day and they are full of stories about and quoted sayings of his friend Scott Fitzgerald. Later Dorothy broke off her engagement to Henry Dunn—a fairly serious thing in the polite society of those days. She went on to marry a Texan and to move out there. Scholars will be relieved to learn that she burned all of her former fiancé's letters. She was not without good memory, though, and she told me a thing or two.

On the other side of the family there was my father's brother, my Uncle Oliver, Oliver H. P. Garrett, a celebrated young newspaperman in New York in the 1920s. Beginning with the advent of sound pictures, he was a screenwriter until his death in the 1950s. He came out of a harder, tougher background. When Fitzgerald and John Biggs and Jim Bettes and other Princeton students got around to answering the call to the colors, Oliver was already in infantry combat against the Germans. He was in the trenches by the fall of 1917. He was wounded and he won the (rare) Distinguished Service Cross and was back home with the war over and behind him before he was old enough to vote. As a reporter he had interviewed Adolph Hitler twice. He knew something of the American underworld, beginning with an exclusive interview with Al Capone and not quite ending when John Dillinger emerged from hiding to see Oliver's movie, *Manhattan Melodrama*, and was killed by the F.B.I. when he came out of the theater. Oliver Garrett, it turned out, knew both Hemingway and Faulkner a little. He is credited with the adaptation of *Sanctuary* (*The Story of Temple Drake*) and with the Gary Cooper-Helen Hayes version of *A Farewell to Arms*, and many more film scripts, both originals and adaptations. His path crossed that of Scott Fitzgerald when Selznick hired Oliver again (he had worked on an earlier version) to write what proved to be the final shooting script for *Gone With the Wind*. Oliver saw and used some of the other scripts that Selznick had bought and paid for. He told me, when I asked about it, that Fitzgerald's scenes were by far the best written of the lot and that the problem for Fitzgerald, as for others, had been Selznick's rigidity about time. He wanted a film of conventional length, and that was simply impossible. Oliver refused to sign on until he was given the freedom to write the film as long as he thought it ought to be.

I don't know, because I never asked, if Oliver Garrett ever actually met and talked to Scott Fitzgerald. I tend to doubt it. There was, however, one other odd connection between the two. Oliver was a close friend, from early on, and at one point a next-door neighbor to Irving Thalberg, the real-life producer on whom Fitzgerald based *The Last Tycoon*. When Thalberg married Norma Shearer, Oliver was an usher at the wedding.

Finally, I might add one more point of connection. My first three books were published by Scribner's where, years later, some of the legend remained, more a matter of haunting than of memory.

So, there was always gossip from the beginning had I been willing and able to ask and to listen. There was also the sometimes acknowledged influence of Fitzgerald's work on many writers of my generation and after. Certainly *Gatsby* has been accorded, among the writers, an almost universal status, by consensus and acclamation, as a masterpiece. And the public image of Fitzgerald has haunted all of us. Conditioned by our expectations, our hopes and fears, we have looked to him for some kind of guidance, positive or negative.

Although a lot of my life has been spent in the Academy, it has seldom involved the teaching of modern and contemporary literature. Thus, I was already in middle age, deep in my own career as a writer and teacher, before I had time and occasion to pause and to think about my own deeply mixed feelings about Fitzgerald. I knew that he was, line by line, move by move, one of the most gifted writers we Americans have ever known. Wescott was right, naming him as the possessor of "the best narrative gift of the century." I also had come to learn, gradually, that Fitzgerald's great elegiac theme of change, change, change, was more prophetic than he could have known or perhaps even wished. Tuned to change, fascinated by its nuances, he feared it as well. As well he might. Whether we recognize it or not, we are now so different in details that we are scarcely connected with his lost time and its ways and means. There is a natural tendency of American artists to imagine themselves as being part of a steady progression, certainly including the previous generation or two. It is clear that Hemingway, Faulkner, Fitzgerald, and many others of their generation believed that they were more or less doing the same thing and that they belonged to the same grand tradition that included, for example, James and Conrad and Meredith. They were wrong about this, but not so much in error as are those of us who came along afterwards and who may believe that we, too, are part of an ongoing progression and tradition including the great modern masters like Fitzgerald. Our calling, in keeping with the society where it is manifested, is radically different from that of our fathers and grandfathers. We cannot learn very many practical details from them and their examples. The world—even the shrinking world of literature—is too different to be justly compared. The same things will not likely happen again. All things are reduced to what Faulkner used to call "the old verities." It is there that Fitzgerald has instructed as well as delighted a whole generation of American writers. Proof of the century's changes is in his work, maybe more than anyone else's. It is from his work that we can most clearly discern where we have been and where we have come from. Ironically, then, his art, which so subtly records change and decay, transcends both.

What are some of the things that living writers are able to learn by calling up the example of Scott Fitzgerald? The great exemplary lessons of his impeccable and inimitable craft are subtle ones and run somewhat counter to the fashions and the forces of these times. His art is more admirable than directly influential. Mainly and more generally, his work teaches that it is possible to be original and innovative without embracing or asserting overt idiosyncrasy; that it is possible to cultivate a true and individual voice without calling an unseemly, self-reflexive attention to the creator. But these are hard lessons, perhaps unavailable, maybe even undesirable to any but the mature artist. It seems to require maturity to be able to appreciate fully Fitzgerald's mature art.

It may be in the example of his vocational life (not his private life, except insofar as it imposes upon the vocational) that he has most to show and tell other writers. I do not mean the easy and obvious lessons, which are, in any case, more a matter of cliché than reality. For instance, Fitzgerald is often cited as a prime example of the catastrophe of early success, followed by a long, frustrated attempt to repeat that achievement. More to the point is the whole career, in the face of many formidable public and private troubles, during which he continued to grow and to develop as an artist and to produce work of the highest quality. He is not at all to be taken as an example of deflected talent and wasted gifts; though he, like anyone else, might well have done more and better work under better circumstances. The important, astonishing thing is how much and how well he performed under often very difficult conditions. One thing, then, that Fitzgerald represents for us who came along afterwards is enormous will-power, which taken together with talent and courage and dedication, allowed him to keep working, creating for as long as he lived. He lives on, with honor, by that example.

Then and Now:
In Cold Blood *Revisited*

Now it is a matter of memory, but then it was an experience. Not simply a memorable event, but an experience lived in and through and worth remembering, one of those rare occurrences that, even after all is said and done, modified and revised by time, can be said to have changed things.

In my house, which is, among other things, a hopeless clutter and chaos of books, placed in no known or discernible order, I can go directly to it, no groping and searching, and lift Truman Capote's *In Cold Blood,* hardcover, first printing, off the shelf. Partly, this is because of the unusual book jacket (slightly torn and frayed since 1965) consisting of nothing but words: title and author on front and spine; on the back, "Books by Truman Capote," a list of his nine published titles at that time, including this one. No blurbs, no photograph, fore or aft. On the end flap, "About the Author," we learn Capote's date of birth—September 30, 1924; that his first novel, *Other Voices, Other Rooms,* "was an international literary success and established the author in the first rank of contemporary writers—a position he has since sustained with additional novels and short stories, as well as his widely praised experiments in the field of reportage." The copy goes on to claim that this new book "represents the culmination of his long-standing desire to make a contribution toward the establishment of a serious new literary form: the Nonfiction Novel."

In an essay review written at the time, I quibbled with that claim, reminding other readers and myself of e. e. cummings's *The Enormous Room*; of Hemingway's *Green Hills of Africa, Death in the Afternoon,* and *A Moveable Feast;* of the whole line of books descending from Walter Lord's *A Night to Remember.* And at that moment I had ignored, and will not again, the major contribution to the form, Shelby Foote's magnificent achievement, *The Civil War: A Narrative,* which, by 1963, was two-thirds done, with the first two volumes in print. All of which only suggests that other writers had thought and were thinking at the same time in the same way—that, somehow, the traditional novel, as it came to them and was practiced, did not have the ways and means to deal honestly and artistically with large events of the past or with the mad reality of our own times, with what Capote described in an interview as "desperate, savage, violent America in collision with sane, safe, insular even smug America— people who have every chance against people who have none." The real world was, they thought, too wild for fiction, but the hard facts of it could be tamed and arranged in a narrative form, what Tom Wolfe would later call "the New Journalism."

The front flap of the jacket is equally spare and unusual, then or now. Title and subtitle, "A True Account of a Multiple Murder and Its Consequences." The text, a little over 100 words, deserves to be quoted in full:

On November 15, 1959, in the small town of Holcomb, Kansas, four members of the Clutter family were savagely murdered by blasts from a shotgun held a few inches from their faces. There was no apparent motive for the crime and there were almost no clues.

Five years, four months and twenty-nine days later, on April 14, 1965, Richard Eugene Hitchcock, aged thirty-three, and Perry Edward Smith, aged thirty-six, were hanged on a gallows in a warehouse in the Kansas State Penitentiary in Lansing, Kansas.

In Cold Blood is the story of the lives and deaths of these six people. It has already been hailed as a masterpiece.

All but the final sentence is made up of bare facts and numbers, might as well be a newspaper account, surprising in its flat tone (only the word "savagely" is an adverbial judgment call) and perhaps surprising in that it might seem to eliminate some of the suspense of the story. We are told what happened to the six principals before opening the book or reading a page.

But we knew that anyway. The last statement on the jacket is factual also. This book had been serialized in *The New Yorker* with great success. In his "Acknowledgments" Capote thanks "Mr. William Shawn of *The New Yorker,* who encouraged me to undertake this project, and whose judgment stood me in good stead from first to last."

I remember that, remember, after the first chunk of it appeared, waiting eagerly for the next issue of *The New Yorker.* People talked about it with excitement in the way that people only talk about good new movies nowadays. I couldn't wait to get my hands on the book. Didn't wait too long, either, to have acquired an expensive ($5.95) hardcover of the first printing. Waiting around for it we read all about Capote and the new book in all the

magazines. I'll never forget the big spread in *Life* magazine where Capote, calm and matter-of-fact, allowed:
"The book will be a classic." And in any case it was a
huge and instantaneous success, a bestseller, a Book-of-
the-Month Club selection (more important then than
now); paperback rights were sold for an enormous sum;
movie rights were promptly purchased.

It's true, Capote had enjoyed a good measure of
literary fame and success ever since the appearance of
Other Voices, Other Rooms; but this was a great leap, a
grande jete into popular success. Fame became celebrity.
Then that celebrity was at once confirmed and flaunted in
1967 by a party at the Plaza Hotel—"The Party," Gloria
Steinem named it in *Vogue* magazine, "a great masked ball
that would bring guests from Europe and Asia, not to
mention Kansas, California, and Harlem"—to which
Capote invited 540 people, enough of them celebrities to
be called (again by Gloria Steinem) "a new Four Hundred
of the World."

What else about the book itself? It is a very hand-
somely made and designed book, beautifully printed on
the best paper and with a rare and elegant full-cloth
binding. Made to last. Made to be kept and appreciated.
Made to tell the world: *This is real class.* Open it up and
you are soon greeted on the title page by a chilling
illustration, the only one in the book or jacket—two pairs
of eyes, an extreme close shot in black and white, the eyes
of the killers, here brooding over the story to follow. To
say the eyes of these two dead young men are haunting
would be understatement. That it is, finally, their book,
their story, is underscored by the epigraph, four lines
asking for pity and God's mercy, from François Villon's
"*Ballade des pendus.*"

One thing more. We soon discover that one of the people to whom the book is dedicated is Capote's old childhood friend Harper Lee, author of *To Kill a Mockingbird,* one of the best-loved stories of our time. From all the advance publicity about the making of the book, we already knew that Harper Lee had helped him in various ways in the research and socially in winning over reticent people in Kansas.

The advance publicity, unusual for the time, and the carefully designed jacket copy for the book served a powerful technical purpose as well. Since we knew, more or less, what was coming to pass before reading the first words on the first page, knew that what was coming was horrific—"blasts from a shotgun held a few inches from their faces," to be followed in due course by a double hanging, Capote was free to do what he did, building his story quietly and inexorably. Building it around a classical four-part structure, he could, paradoxically, keep suspense at a high level throughout. The first three sections move along quickly and easily, intercutting back and forth between the murderers and their unsuspecting victims, then the hunters and the hunted. In the final section, "The Corner," dealing with the trial and punishment, Capote demonstrated a virtuoso magician's sleight of hand. By now all the original suspense has been dissipated, and the announced conclusion, the hanging of the killers, was obligatory. Yet he managed to get there without any diminishment of intensity or interest. The hanging scene is one of the finest of its kind, right up there with Melville's *Billy Budd* and the hanging of Popeye in William Faulkner's *Sanctuary.* With one great difference. Melville and Faulkner scrupulously avoided the dramatic clichés, working against the grain of the material. Capote pulled out all the stops: "The hangman coughed—impatiently lifted his cowboy hat and settled it again, a gesture somehow reminiscent of a turkey buzzard huffing, then smoothing its neck feathers—and Hickcock, nudged by an attendant, mounted the scaffold steps." That others present at the scene recalled the details, including the condemned men's last words, differently is not strictly relevant. It's a hell of a hanging.

Before *In Cold Blood,* Capote had written—in *Other Voices, Other Rooms, The Grass Harp,* even in the light-hearted *Breakfast at Tiffany's*—romantic fables, well-removed from the world of "realistic" fiction. Even though each of these works is different from the others, all have a clear and consistent moral frame, an inversion of conventional, middle-class values. Even the lovable Holly Golightly of *Breakfast at Tiffany's* has a hard and independent core: "Good? Honest is more what I mean. Not low-type honest—I'd rob a grave, I'd steal two-bits off a dead man's eyes if I thought it would contribute to the day's enjoyment—but unto-thyself-type honest. Be anything but a coward, a pretender, an emotional crook, a whore: I'd rather have cancer than a dishonest heart." In each of these books, and most of the short stories, it is the outsiders and the outcasts who reject conventional morality and are examples of another kind of virtue. Those who manage to prosper or get along in the duplicitous world of practical matters are usually exposed as being, at heart, deceitful and/or self-deceived, hypocrites at best. It is these, too, who make real mischief and cause real trouble. In the end, thanks to a kind of whimsical Providence or poetic justice, they get what is coming to them.

In *In Cold Blood* it is the all-American Clutter family—Herbert William Clutter, forty-eight, the father; Bonnie, his wife; Kenyon, fifteen, the only son; and Nancy, sixteen, "the town darling"—whom destiny has selected to represent, in Capote's telling, "sane, safe, insular, even smug America—people who have every chance against people who have none." Anyone at all familiar with the world of Capote's earlier fiction knew two things, why he had chosen this subject and not another, and what doom was coming to the Clutters, from the moment he first introduced Herbert Clutter. "Always certain of what he wanted in the world, Mr. Clutter had in large measure obtained it." Poor Clutter is even physically emblematic of the doom-deserving, vulnerable losers (outward and visible winners) of Capote's universe: "Though he wore rimless glasses and was of but average height, standing just under five feet ten, Mr. Clutter cut a man's-man figure. His shoulders were broad, his hair had held its dark color, his square-jawed confident face retained a healthy-hued youthfulness, and his teeth, unstained and strong enough to shatter walnuts, were still intact." People who happened to have read Capote would read that passage and others with an awareness of his irony. People who had never read a word until the arrival of *In Cold Blood*, the huge majority of the audience that made the book a bestseller, were at once invited and allowed to take things straight, at face value. The subtext, however, is slightly camouflaged and complicated because there are some good "straights" in the story, the most important of whom, "a lean and handsome fourth-generation Kansan of forty-seven," is Alvin Adams Dewey, an agent of the Kansas Bureau of Investigation and the closest facsimile of a conventional "hero" in the book. Alvin Dewey and his family became friends of Capote in real life and was noted by Gloria Steinem in her account of "The Party" in 1967. "Alvin Dewey answered questions about problems of the Clutter case, just as dignified and direct in the Paley dining room as he had been in Kansas during the murder investigation in *In Cold Blood*." Subtext: *There are some real people out there beyond the Hudson, Dorothy. Even in a place like Kansas.* But Dewey, as a figure in the book, is treated with a respect and consideration that, otherwise, only the killers receive.

Capote is adroitly clever here, too. He inverts the old good-cop bad-cop convention and uses it on the murderers. One, Dick Hickcock, is from the outset the most blameworthy and the least attractive, basically a bad influence on the other, Perry Smith, who is presented with deeply dimensional sympathy. Hickcock is the heavy. There is an archetypal malevolence about him with his head "halved like an apple, then put together a fraction off center," with his "left eye being truly serpentine, with a venomous, sickly-blue squint that, although it was involuntarily acquired, seemed nevertheless to warn of bitter sediment at the bottom of his nature." That's our first impression. Not too pretty, huh? You bring a serpent and an apple together in the same paragraph and you're talking Original Sin and suchlike.

Perry Smith, though he suffers from a physical deformity as the result of an accident, has an interesting look about him: "It was a changeling's face, and mirror-guided experiments had taught him how to ring the changes, how to look now ominous, now impish, now soulful; a tilt of the head, a twist of the lips, and the corrupt gypsy became the gentle romantic." Perry Smith becomes, in almost every detail we are given, a spooky embodiment of Capote's early fiction. What could be more perfect for a Capote protagonist than to be the child of "a lean Cherokee girl [who] rode a wild horse, a 'bucking bronco,' and her loosened hair whipped back and forth, flew about like a flamenco dancer's"? Capote gives us an empathetic and fascinating look at a murderer's psyche through his portrait of Perry Smith.

There are a number of problems, more evident in hindsight than at the time. For one thing, there is the complex matter of fact and judgment. When pictures of the people involved appeared in the magazines, it was clear how many of Capote's descriptions and judgments were subjective, *literary*. The people did not look much like the people he described. Later it turned out that they did not do or say all the things he attributed to them; and some things neither he nor anyone else could have known. Still, it was wonderful reporting and charged writing. And we have become used to the other flaws in our post-Capote nonfiction narratives.

There is also the slightly more disturbing fact that neither the Clutters nor the killers were fictional constructs. They were real people. The brains and blood and hair that splatter walls of the house at River Valley Farm were real. There remains the often asked and always unanswered question, then: Were the lives and deaths of these people exploited for the sake of our titillation and the author's profit? Maybe so, but by now both titillation and profit from the real sufferings of others have become so commonplace as to leave us unfit to ask that question about a book from thirty-one years ago. Maybe Capote lent to the "true crime" story a patina of literary respectability; but now it seems that this was coming anyway, part of the spirit of the 1960s, as was our gradual changeover from concern for victims to fascination with perpetrators. Capote's book had something to do with that change of heart and values and certainly spawned a multitude of literary imitations in both fiction and nonfiction. For that reason alone, *In Cold Blood* is an important book, a historical landmark. And, finally, there is another, maybe stronger claim the book makes. The "real" world of America as revealed in this story, of which Capote said at the time "It's what I really think about America," has come to pass, and is far more a matter of public fact than private vision. Who today would deny that we live in a "desperate, savage, violent America [that is] in collision with sane, safe, insular, even smug America"? In that sense, *In Cold Blood* can qualify as prophecy.

What was beyond prophecy, even predictability, was that this book would be the last "big" book by Truman Capote. There would be five more books in his lifetime, none without style and merit, but none of them more than minor exercises. When he died in 1984, he had been working for many years on the novel *Answered Prayers*, dealing with his rich and powerful acquaintances, the folks who came to The Party. When something was cobbled together by Random House from published excerpts and leftover bits and pieces, it was described on the jacket as "perhaps the most famous unpublished novel in contemporary American letters." The publication of *Answered Prayers* in 1987 did little or nothing to change that judgment call. Meantime, no question about it, Truman Capote's continuing claim on our attention derives from and rests in an single extraordinary volume—*In Cold Blood*.

Miss Eudora When Last Seen

It would have been in late 1947 or early 1948, most likely the latter because there is a blizzard in the story and I remember the blizzard as being early in the new year (1948).

Anyway, the war was over and I had gone north to go to college (Princeton) and, except for football season during which I was trying and pretending to be a player, I spent as much time as I could in New York City, an hour away from Princeton. I had friends there, grown-ups who were fun to be with, and one of them was a beautiful painter from my hometown who was kind and hospitable. I went to see her as often as I could in those days.

At Princeton I had just discovered Southern literature. I had my brand-new, neat, fat little *Viking Portable Faulkner,* which was my prize possession. I also had a paperback copy of Carson McCullers's *The Heart is a Lonely Hunter,* given to me by the painter.

I had not yet heard of Eudora Welty, but on a weekend in the city I found and bought two of her books—*A Curtain of Green* (1941) and *The Wide Net* (1942). I missed *The Robber Bridegroom* (1942), which would later (soon enough) become my absolute special favorite, and I missed *Delta Wedding* (1946), too, at that time.

I bought the two story collections on the weekend of the big blizzard just as the first few harmless flakes were falling. It would have to be late Friday afternoon, then. I did not buy the books at the Gotham Book Mart as you might expect. I can't give you the name of the store. It was new and fancy and Swedish (I think), somewhere among the other bright and new and fancy façades of Fifth Avenue or maybe Madison. They had mostly art books for sale. Only a few, a very few, literary items in stock. I browsed, picked up a Welty, opened at random, read a couple or three sentences and knew at once and for sure that I wanted everything they had, up to the limits of the cash I was carrying, by this Welty person.

Bought those books and read and reread them, with enormous pleasure and excitement, that very weekend when I was, finally, snowbound in a walk-up apartment, albeit with good company, in Greenwich Village. At some point a small group of us, painters and musicians and the college kid, walked in fresh knee-deep snow up the middle of Fifth Avenue. Except for us, it was almost empty, only a few people darkly wrapped against the cold and no vehicles, nary a one, of any kind, not even a snowplow. Back inside, the little apartment warmed in places by the burners of a gas cooking stove, I curled up with Eudora Welty. Changed my life and changed my luck. (As they say.) As a reader—I knew then and there that I would be reading and rereading her work the rest of my life with joy and undiminishing excitement. And as a writer—because that is what I had always wanted to be if I couldn't be a fireman, a steeplejack, or a locomotive engineer—she opened doors and windows for me, set an impeccable example, not to be *copied*, which I couldn't even if I wanted and tried to, but to admire and strive to be worthy of. Which did not mean, then or now, that I sought her approval for my work, which (as you'll see a little later) I could not have earned in any case if that had been my wish. Instead, and much more important to a learning writer, she challenged me, and any other new writer, young or old, challenged us all to do nothing less than our best.

What about technique? You might well ask. You know, tricks of the trade.

Well now, that's another story. Of course, there are good things of the kind that any writer can learn from close study of Welty's work. No doubt. But the truth is, the truly amazing thing, that again and again in her stories (novels too) there is a totally inexplicable moment of pure unadulterated and inimitable magic. I mean real magic, because there is no technical or mechanical explanation for it. Take a good look sometime at that great story, "Powerhouse," I dare you, and see if you can really figure out how she did it, how she got from here to there and back.

If it is magic, then what can the writer learn? Answer: to work without ceasing and to be ready, always, for the arrival of angels and magic when and if they elect to come. You can learn technique from lesser beings. You learn craft from honest and honorable craftsmen. From a few, the very few, including Eudora Welty, you learn to recognize and rejoice in art when you see it. From Eudora Welty you learn to believe in magic.

I knew all that and more after my snowbound weekend with two books by Eudora Welty.

⚬

I have been with Eudora Welty in person on a number of occasions, at a number of conferences, celebrations, panels and so forth, mostly down South, though once in far off North Dakota. (What we were all doing there, I can't imagine.) And it has always been a great pleasure, thanks to her generous and gracious manner, her wit and good humor, her integrity and her sharp tongue. For this latter she has not been sufficiently credited. Call it part of a tough-minded vision. She is not in the least sentimental, in life or art. She is unfailing in her compassion for others.

I was not, have never been, one of her good and close friends in a social sense. It seemed from day one until now that she was spoken for (as they say). There were many other writers—William Jay Smith, Walker Percy, Reynolds Price, Peter Taylor, Richard Ford, Barry Hannah—who were around and about her in a social sense as good friends. She didn't need another writer in her train. If she ever did, of course, I would have swallowed shyness and abjured my clumsiness and done my dead level best to serve.

Way back when, when my first collection of stories, *King of the Mountain,* was published, somebody, a mutual friend, sent her a copy. Shortly thereafter she sent him a postcard thanking him, saying she had much enjoyed the first story in the book, "The Rivals," and was looking forward to the others. I didn't hear from him again for a good while, years in fact. When I did run into him somewhere, I asked if he had ever heard any more from Miss Welty about the rest of the book. "Too much ugly talk," he said. "She said there was too much ugly talk in some of the others." Were my feelings hurt? Not a bit. I was charmed and enchanted. I knew well enough the stories she referred to; they were my Army stories and in some of them people did indeed indulge in "ugly talk." My mother, a few years older than Eudora Welty, agreed with Welty about that, though being a Southern mother, she defended me without stint or hesitation in her book club and her bridge club.

Truth is, I wouldn't have sent the book to Miss Welty myself. It seemed an imposition and I saw and still see no good reason why she should have to read stories (be they good or bad or indifferent) about tacky people in the U.S. Army. You could look at it this way: one of the reasons we were in the U.S. Army was to spare people like Miss Welty and my mother from the ugly talk of an ugly world.

With a little age and experience, I probably wouldn't have wanted to shock folks with my Army stories. With some wisdom, I might have realized that I couldn't shock them anyway. They (and she) knew the world as well or better than I.

Many years later, with panels and conferences and such in between, I enjoyed a most pleasant time in her company when she came to Charlottesville to visit old friends and, while she was here, to give a reading to raise some money for a literacy program. It was arranged for four of us to read on the program—myself, Rita Mae Brown, Ann Beattie, and the featured star, Miss Welty. I read first and as briefly as possible, something from one of the Elizabethan novels with not a smidgen of ugly talk. Read and sat down next to Miss Welty, noticing that she had a copy of the Modern Library edition of *Selected Stories of Eudora Welty* in hand. It was somewhat battered and certainly well-thumbed. From time to time, she stole a glance at it, checking the text. She was, I was pleased to notice, as nervous as the rest of us, really, maybe more so. After all this time. After years of reading to audiences. I took it as an act of duty, assumed that she didn't really enjoy standing up and showing off her art and craft; but there was nothing but to do it.

The story she was glancing at, from time to time, was "A Worn Path." The margins were marked with little notes to herself. I'm pretty sure that one read: "Slow Down!"

Rita Mae Brown rose and read something that was supposed to be funny and did, indeed, arouse some laughter in the audience. Miss Welty, next to me, sighed a deep sigh. Then Ann Beattie rose and read a very funny piece evoking much laughter. In the midst of this Miss Welty sighed a deeper sigh and then began riffling pages, looking for something. Just as Ann Beattie finished, Miss Welty found "Why I Live at the P.O.," rose and moved to the lectern to read it. Over her head, like a balloon in a comic strip, I saw clearly the entirely imaginary words— "You girls want to be funny. I'll give you funny." And it was wonderfully funny, the best I've ever heard her read it. The audience was, as they say, in stitches.

Later that weekend the president of the University of Virginia gave a luncheon for Miss Welty at the French House where they practice the French language and lifestyle. Various students and faculty (including lucky me) were invited. It was a really good meal with great wines and conversation and went on into the middle of the afternoon. It was there that I learned Miss Welty was blessed with a hearty appetite, worthy of one of our football players, if truth has to be known. She was about to eat a second dessert when her host and friend spoke up. "Eudora," he said, "it's after three already and we are due for dinner at Monticello at five or five-thirty. . . ."

"Five-thirty!" she said. "By five-thirty I'll be hungry as a bear."

I am happy to join in this tribute and celebration for the ninetieth birthday of Eudora Welty. She and her work have been part of my life for half a century. Which, while it can't compete with ninety, is still a big chunk of time.

Consider: how many writers have kept your attention and given you nothing but joy for fifty years?

The last time I saw Miss Welty was at a meeting of the Fellowship of Southern Writers (of which she is a charter member) in Chattanooga where she was to receive an award. More or less by accident it fell my duty and pleasure to escort her onto the stage, from backstage, at the theater where the ceremony took place. With Miss Welty holding my arm we stepped out of shadowy darkness into a sudden blinding blaze of light and an animal roar of applause. The crowd, a couple of thousand or more, was on its feet cheering and clapping.

"How do you like this, Miss Welty?" I asked.

She gave me a brief and lovely smile.

"If they keep it up," she said, "I just might have to cry."

We are going to keep it up, Miss Welty.

A Day's Fair Work: Observations on the Poetry of Fred Chappell

All in all, it's been a day's fair work.
　　　　　—Epilogue to *Spring Garden*

These modern days
We're all a bunch of cowbirds, you know that?
　　　　　—"Remodeling the Hermit's Cabin"

High in my expensive hotel room, on a gray chilly day in the city of Chicago, I am reading and rereading, with deep and intense pleasure and with a little minor pain, Fred Chappell's *Spring Garden: New and Selected Poems*. There is a good club sandwich on the table nearby and a green bottle of Heineken, both of which are violations of my regular hometown diet. But here I am, far from home.

Did you hear me right? Did I say pain? I said, "a little minor pain." My admiration for all these poems, this book, the art and craft of it all, the intelligence and wisdom, is overwhelming—but not without a little of the old pepper, the bitter spice of envy. I would have given anything to conceive and execute it. Not every poet I know of in this sad and brutal and duplicitous age where we find ourselves, like it or not, would want or would try to write this book, these poems, even if they somehow magically possessed the ability to do so. Most of them would not dare to fly in the face of current literary fashions, to risk a turning away from the by-now safe and secure, familiar contemporary trends and tropes. Mostly they prefer the spotlit supermodel strut on the runway, moving to the rowdy and primitive rhythms of rap and rock-and-roll, to the ancient and honorable enterprise (celebrated metaphorically by Yeats long years ago) of going and being naked. Or as Chappell and Virgil will have it in *Plowing Naked*. Chappell's art is, in fact, much more like that of Salome or of Gypsy Rose Lee or of Sally Rand, with her deft fans and balloons, than, say, that of Claudia Schiffer or Linda Evangelista caught in the perpetual summer lightning of flashbulbs and celebrity.

The book, *Spring Garden*, is in my hands, its handsome, multicolored jacket featuring the subtle earth and green tones of Albrecht Durer, a rich tangle of fecundity. The book itself is bound partly in black cloth and in a splendid cardboard of gold and black, spattered flecks against a ground of dark green, serving to echo the colors and the excitement of the jacket and, perhaps, suggesting a starry sky, one of the persistent images of the poems.

The book is roughly nine by six inches, and its contents weigh seventeen ounces. Open the book and what you will find is ninety-six poems from a lifetime (so far), rigorously selected from among many more, many others, some of these uncollected, others chosen as representative of the work in nine individual collections, not counting any number of chapbooks.

A selected poems is, among other things, a modest request for recognition and definition. The poems here are arranged in seven subtitled sections: "In the Garden," "The Good Life," "The Garden of Love," "Poems of Character," "Poems of Fantasy," "Epigrams," and "Poems of Memory," each of these sections being presented with a newly written introductory poem, and the whole volume bracketed by an expansive, stanzaic "Prologue" and "Epilogue," which, among a number of other things, establish and then maintain the garden of the title in its two principal forms—first, as a "real" garden, the one in Greensboro, North Carolina, designed and tended by the poet's wife, Susan Chappell, and much enjoyed and exploited by the poet in reality; and second, as a metaphorical garden, the immemorial garden celebrated by poets of all times, the garden of Chaucer and Spenser and Ronsard and DuBellay, the garden that also stands for art.

It is, then, a carefully structured book, aiming at and for a good deal more than a conventional anthology arrangement of diverse poems. This should not be surprising. All of Chappell's books of poems since the making of the four volumes that constitute *Mid-Quest* (1981) have been carefully structured as books, not modeled on the art gallery or the musical review, but plotted in sequence to form a general aesthetic experience, not only poem by poem, but with each poem seeking its proper place in the larger design. Which is the larger, imaginary poem in somewhat the same sense that Dante's comedy is known as *La Poema* while all other poems are identified as *La Poesia*. Chappell's poems, in all of their various guises and disguises, move and dance in the setting, the context of a larger architecture. Real and imaginary figures move together precisely in a real and an imaginary garden.

On the same elegant book jacket for *Spring Garden* we have the words of John Lang, lifted from *The Oxford Companion to Twentieth Century Poetry*, a blurb, then, at once useful and pertinent to a book of selected poems, although, as is the case with any well-meant appreciative commentary (including this one of my own), it is by definition bound to be much oversimplified and inadequate. Lang writes:

> Chappell's art derives from two major sources: his childhood and youth in the Appalachian mountains

and his wide reading in the books, philosophical as
well as literary, that have shaped Western culture.
Among the most notable qualities of his poetry are its
carefully crafted variety of forms, its fine storytelling
and creation of character, its humor, and its serious
moral intent. Chappell's poems reveal both enormous
erudition and a profound commitment to what he
has called "folk art."

A thoughtful and intelligent piece of general criticism.
Some of the things it leaves out or, anyway, does not
explicitly mention. For example, that the autobiographical intent is not by any means limited to
childhood and youth, but continues into maturity. That
fantasy in a variety of kinds and forms has always been
a part of Chappell's poetry. That he is a master of the
ancient and honorable (and increasingly rare) love
poem. But Lang's remarks are a good beginning. And so
are those of poet and translator and novelist David
Slavitt in the *Dictionary of Literary Biography Yearbook
1995*. Which, by the way, gave to Chappell's *Spring
Garden* their award for a Distinguished Volume of
Poetry Published in 1995. Writing about *Spring Garden,*
Slavitt reports:

> This is not only a retrospective volume of the first
> order from a poet who, despite a Bollingen Prize, is
> less well known than he ought to be, but it is an
> innovative and fascinating way of presenting the work
> of a career. With a flutter of the fedora in the
> direction of Ronsard, Chappell gives us a graceful
> general prologue and an epilogue that serve as a
> context so that the poems, rearranged and reordered
> as he has them here, become a kind of auto-
> biography, a recollection and reconsideration of a life

in writing. Chappell has the finesse and poise to carry
it off with great panache. It is an extraordinary book,
an ornament not merely of the year but of the
decade.

A little later, Slavitt goes on to say: "Chappell, I have
believed for years, is one of the best poets alive writing
in English."

I would here add to that altogether acceptable
judgment a qualifier of my own: that Chappell is one of
maybe half a dozen living poets writing in our language
who is a true master of prosody and metrics. Never
mind the self-advertisements of so many of the
neoformalists. Since the death of O. B. Hardison, Jr.,
Chappell stands among the diminishing number of
American poets who can work well and easily in the
tightest and most complex verse forms (as well as the
lightest) in such a way that, for the life of the poem, you
can safely believe, without doubt or question, the poet's
pretense that we really and truly can think and speak
that way—extemporaneously. The poem and its form
appear to be happening at the given moment of reading.

In addition to fluent mastery of prosody—a mastery
that allows for a perfected free verse whenever he and his
subject require it, Chappell's poems are extremely interesting technically. Other elements that serve to make the
music of poetry are richly omnipresent. This whole piece
could well be devoted to Chappell's subtle verbal texture
or to his adroit use of rhyme—internal and end rhymes,
consonantal and assonantal rhymes and echoes, adventures and exploits with feminine rhyming. Take, for
example, the second and final stanza of Chappell's bleak
depiction of the "ordinary" urban scene in "Score":

The midnight of the needle
And the nickel. The fairway suburbs send

Their shaken daughters out to wheedle
The ominous stranger and habitual friend.
She delivers her snowy intelligence;
Her empty eyes declare
A whole Manhattan of indifference,
A whole Miami of despair.

The usual effect (in English) of feminine end rhyme—
needle/wheedle, intelligence/indifference (and even the
internal half-rhyme of needle/nickel)—is cheerful and
almost always comic or satirical in effect and intention.
But here they are deadly serious and dangerous. Rhymes
like hand grenades.

None of which is to say or to suggest that Chappell is
in any sense an old-fashioned poet. Only that he is boldly
willing to risk that misapprehension even as he summons
up our buried and sometimes ignored, if not forgotten,
tradition like a benign ghostmaster. The risk, however, is
not as great as it might seem. Nobody that I can think
of—not the late James Merrill nor anyone from the list of
distinguished Aiken-Taylor Award winners, Wilbur and
Hecht and Nemerov and Nims, for example, none of
them is as easy and fluent in such a variety of forms as
Chappell. Nobody else that I know of has acquired the art
of speaking in such a variety of voices; the chorus and
choir become his own. Part of Chappell's unique voice is
the range of his rhetoric, from high style to the colloquial
and idiomatic, that he can present often in the selfsame
poem. Chappell can perform this rare ventriloquist's trick
without evident strain or any false notes. Some other
poets, some of us, have tried to do just that, partly in
answer to the extreme specialization and the deliberate
limitations of voice that characterize so much contemporary American poetry. Many have tried and are still trying.
Fred Chappell has already succeeded.

In this volume, for example, he speaks to us directly

in the voices of Fred Chappell—husband, poet, reader, and dreamer; but as well, in the elegantly incorporated translations, in the voices of (among others) Ronsard, Charles d'Orleans, Baudelaire, Verlaine, Horace and Martial and Statius, Petrarch, even the Emperor Hadrian whose pretty little poem is, if I may say so, much improved even as it is revived.

And as for characters, the people he presents, credible and fully dimensional, the range of them is wide and inclusive—men and women and children of all ages; baseball players and artists; hermits and lovers; mountain folk, talking scarecrows, mythological creatures, figures lifted out of fairy tales; and even a living, breathing, and talking story.

Something else bears mention. That Chappell is also (in the Southern tradition perhaps best exemplified by the late Robert Penn Warren) a first-rate novelist and storywriter, a recognized and honored creator of fiction that matters as fiction. His seventh novel, *Farewell, I'm Bound to Leave You*, has recently appeared and received glowing reviews. There is also Chappell's criticism, which, without loss of objectivity and with no discernible diminishment of rigor, celebrates what is worthy and well made while glaring, unblinking, at all that is pretentious and spurious. Some of Chappell's critical work, a small but representative selection, is gathered in *Plow Naked: Selected Writings on Poetry* (1993). Much more of his criticism, including a great many significant book reviews, remains to be collected and published. But even from what we have available now, there are general things worth noticing: That he has no ideological guide to poetry and, as he puts it, "I have not been able to hold to abstract, fixed standards." That he refuses to be rigidly consistent, because his chief concern is not primarily critical nor exclusively theoretical, but rather takes the stance of a receptive reader. He writes that "each separate work of art implies its own aesthetic principles and I take the discovery and elucidation of these to be part of the job of a receptive reader."

Among the working writers of our era, Chappell has made his indelible mark in all these forms—poetry, fiction, criticism. Our proper subject here is the poetry. But I must at least suggest that there is a fruitful field for inquiry and study of the kinship (likeness and differences) of his poetry and fiction. How the two play off against each other and nourish each other. And another thing: Chappell has been a teacher for more than a generation. In addition to creative writing, he has taught literature and film and has exercised considerable influence on many students. Though he is quick to satirize and even to ridicule the worst academic bad habits, he is also in the right place and *milieu* for the kind of intellectual life he has cultivated, what he refers to in the epilogue as "My happy studies in ancient poetry / In French, in the Italian Renaissance / In science, religion, and philosophy."

Technically the poet Fred Chappell is the equal of anybody else in the game (and the master of most), in long and short poems and, as well, in the structuring of them into larger designs like *Mid-Quest* and *Spring Garden*. But beyond these things there is what he has to say, the things he chooses to celebrate, what he honors or condemns. The poetry itself is, in St. Augustine's term, the cortex, which like nutshell and nut, contains a nucleus, a center of meaning that likewise, even in our assertively nonjudgmental age, is what we finally judge and value most in first-rate poetry. Chaucer (and others) called the two elements the *sense,* the outward and visible words and form of the poem, and the *sentence*, the meaning, the matter. It is meet and right to consider the *sentence* of Fred Chappell's poetry. St. Augustine said, and poets for more than a thousand years never saw any good reason to question the validity of his statement, that the purpose of poetry was to tell the truth—truth being *caritas* (charity), the love and peace that pass all understanding. Its opposite is *cupiditas* (sin), which blooms brightly in the false garden, in the soil of untruth. This beautiful simplicity is complicated by the shifty and constantly shifting, mutating shapes of appearance and reality and by the fact that any poetry can contain this meaning. It cannot exist separately from the poem. It lives in and from the poem.

⊷═◉═⊶

Coming home on Amtrak, on the Capital Limited, Chicago to Washington D.C.

Yesterday, at the Newberry Library, Richard Wilbur received the T. S. Eliot Award from the Ingersoll Foundation. Fred Chappell received the T. S. Eliot Award in 1993, joining a baker's dozen of distinguished prize-winners, including (among others) Jorge Luis Borges, Anthony Powell, Eugene Ionesco, V. S. Naipaul, Walker Percy, Octavio Paz, Mario Vargas Llosa, Muriel Spark. Chappell has earned other exemplary and enviable recognition, including, for instance, the Bollingen Prize and an award from the *Académie française*. One need not turn to an inquiry on the subject of Chappell's literary reputation to wonder why it is, though he has received a goodly share of recognition and earned the right to be taken most seriously, that he has not taken his appropriate place in the full range of anthologies and critical studies of contemporary poetry in America. But there is a legitimate question. Which is why the literary establishment has been so slow and so reluctant to recognize Chappell's achievement in poetry.

I sit in my roomette, holding the book, *Spring Garden*, in my hands. Outside the sky is all rags and tatters of gray. Mountains on both sides, crowded with picked-clean trees, all bones now, everything the color of fallen leaf and turned earth, what the Scots call sad brown. Dark streams with sudden lapping and splashing of white water. Here and there, like a dark green blaze, there is a stand of pines or firs. Crossroads and small towns, lopsided frame houses surrounded by rusting cars and tractors, steeples of little churches. As the train slowly passes, a lone man in shirtsleeves in a small brick bank building rises from his desk and comes over to the window, looks and waves. Hopper might have painted him. Chappell could give him a voice.

I am here but I am also elsewhere in Chappell's real and imaginary garden, listening to him, what he has to say and sing.

The getters and spenders, the givers and takers who, with a politician's kind of demented rectitude and a fugitive urgency, try to preserve and defend, to maintain the literary establishment, were clearly troubled when, out of the blue from their point of view, Chappell received the Bollingen Award. I think now that this reaction was a true reflection of the threat that many poets and critics felt, not at the dazzling talent and technical virtuosity of the poems, but at the inner *sentence* of them. One of the great problems we face in much contemporary American poetry is in its trendy insistence on a central core of unearned nihilism. Poets in the Gulag have written with more hope and even good cheer than many of our most honored suburban bards. Chappell plays a different burden, another tune. His view is as unflinching and as critical as any I know of when he considers our peculiar vices and follies and cruelties. But even in the purest fantasy, as in the fabulous and savage world of *Castle Tzingal*, there is a humane consciousness by which to measure and to judge.

Because Chappell is a lifetime reader, ceaselessly curious, there is more than Lang's "erudition" in his work. He is one of our most sophisticated writers, bringing to his work a restless intelligence disciplined by deep study. I believe that this intellectual sophistication, often worn as lightly as that of Robert Frost, has confused, perhaps even outraged, poets who confuse sophistication with cleverness, as they confuse fashion with tradition. Chappell's intelligence and sophistication are a serious cultural threat to those who have profited from a public stance of inward and spiritual emptiness.

There is an irrepressible sanity at the heart of Chappell's poems. Although he can, in the tradition of Martial, wound to the quick with a satirical epigram, he is mostly considerate and compassionate, a moral man of good will. Clearly, he hates and speaks out against cruelty, hypocrisy, pride and arrogance, big and little lies. He ridicules powerful delusions and frozen stereotypes. He celebrates fidelity, humility, the powers of love, the honor of a job well done. Here, in "The Stories," in three long lines he says it all in images:

> The story of lovers torn apart by war is a thousand
> pages long.
>
> The story of lovers whom money separates fills all the stiff
> ledgers of Europe.
>
> By the light of a single candle I read the tale of lovers
> grown old together, climbing faithfully to the darkened
> landing of the stairway.

As much as the elder poet, Richard Wilbur, Chappell celebrates and illuminates the things of this world—good wines, good cheese, good food, painting and music, all the lively arts, the small thing seen and known and admired for itself, as here in "Nettle":

> As common as air,
> Startling as fire.

In his introductory poem for the "The Good Life" section of *Spring Garden,* in the fifth stanza, he states it quite explicitly:

> And this Good Life, as I portray it here,
> Consists in steady work and fortitude,
> Of worthy books and modest quietude,
> Science and art, of noble things that were
> And are to be—along with naughtiness
> Of the tame domestic sort, and speculation
> About the lives of ancients, a friendly glass
> Or two: fit objects for proper admiration.

Just so, in "Patience," subtitled "a prologue to *The Georgics,*" he brings together a clash of hopes and fears:

> Total
> War throughout the globe, justice and injustice
> Confounded, every sort of knavery, the plow
> Disused unhonored, the farmer conscripted and his scythe
> Straitly misshapen to make a cruel sword.

But in the end that poem arrives at its destination safely and wisely:

> But nothing changes. The war grinds over the world and all
> Its politics, the soldiers marry the farmers' daughters
> And tell their plowman sons about the fight at the
>   Scaean Gate,
> And other sanguine braveries the dust has eaten.
> Sundown still draws the chickens to their purring roost,
> The cow to the milking stall, the farmer to his porch
>   to watch
> If the soaring constellations promise rain.

Liar, Liar, Pants on Fire: Some Notes on the Life and Art of the Late James Dickey

The main burden of Henry Hart's recently published *James Dickey: The World as a Lie* (Picador), coming to the reading public after eight years of intensive research and investigation, is two-fold: to set a highly inaccurate record straight, and to establish a factual and critical basis for future examinations of the poet's life and art. It was not an easy job, though Hart could not have known that at the outset. He began his task with great interest in his subject and with an understanding and appreciation of Dickey's literary art, particularly the accomplishments of his earlier years, and he emerges from the experience of writing the biography with that sense of honor undiminished by the story he has to tell. Reviewing the book (favorably) in the *Atlanta Journal-Constitution* (April 16, 2000), Stephen Ennis describes the principal problem Hart faced and his answer to it: "Hart devotes much of this biography to disentangling the web of distortion, lies, poses and sheer bluster that Dickey relished. We learn, for example, that Dickey was never the pro football prospect he sometimes claimed to have been. Nor did he serve as a combat pilot during World War II. He did not fly over Nagasaki hours after the dropping of the atomic bomb, and he was never awarded a Purple Heart. He did not play guitar for the country music band the Brazos Valley Boys, nor was he the accomplished hunter and outdoorsman he pretended to be. On the contrary, he shot only one animal in his entire life—a possum—and, according to Hart, 'that may have been fanciful, too.'" What we have in the world of fact is, then, a jock without much talent or ability, a hunter with maybe one kill (maybe it was a roadkill) in a lifetime, a pilot who never flew an airplane after washing out of preliminary flight training, a boozer and unreconstructed womanizer who was mostly impotent when push came to shove, and a major American poet whose best poems were a marvelous achievement and a huge influence on other American poets ever since.

Each reader will find his own favorite anecdotes. Mine involves Dickey as political pundit bombarding Jimmy Carter, in 1976 and 1977, with unsolicited letters of advice and counsel. His advice just before a debate with Gerald Ford—"You might, for example, say something about the recent exploration on Mars which seems conclusively to prove that there is no life on the place where we most hoped it might be discovered"—could have settled the election on the spot.

When I was hired by the University of South Carolina to come there (from Hollins College) and to teach creative writing and literature, I accepted the offer and firmed up the deal (salary, teaching load, etc.) with various deans and with Calhoun Winton, the head of the English Department. Shook hands all around and was ready and eager to drive back to Roanoke, Virginia.

"Before you leave, George," Winton told me, "you probably ought to drop by and see Jim Dickey and say hello. At least let him know you are coming here in the fall."

I agreed. It certainly would be the right thing to do. Winton had known Jim well for many years, going back to Vanderbilt days when they had both been graduate students. And, as it happened, Winton and I had also once upon a time been students together at Princeton. Old boy network in action. . . .

Dickey was right in the big middle of the *Deliverance* experience. The novel had been a best seller and now they were getting ready to shoot the movie down in north Georgia that summer. Part of the reason they had moved to hire me was that they had to have somebody to replace him, or, anyway, to back him up while he was actively involved with the filming and promotion of *Deliverance*. I had known Dickey for a good while, too, and, in fact, I had hired him to be on the poetry staff (along with Richard Wilbur, Henry Taylor, James Seay, Jim White-head, and others) at the previous summer's Hollins Conference in Creative Writing and Cinema. We had never been what you might call—if you were another Southerner of our generation—close buddies. But we got along just fine.

So I drove out from the university into shady residential Columbia and parked in front of Dickey's sprawling ranch-style house nicely situated on the shore of an artificial lake—Lake Katherine. I found Dickey sitting out on his dock enjoying the afternoon sun and the breeze off the water. He invited me to pull up a chair and join him. He offered me a drink, but I think we both settled for tall glasses of iced tea instead. After a little light-hearted small talk he came right to the point.

"George, I understand you are looking for a job here."

"Well, yes, I guess I am."

"I'll do everything I possibly can for you," he said. "I don't know if I can swing it, but I will sure enough do the best I can for you."

"Thanks."

"It would be fun working together. I'm tight, I'm close friends with the president; so, even if the deans and the department don't really want you, I think I might be able to work out something anyway."

"Yes."

"How much money are you thinking about?"

All these years later I don't have even the ghost of a memory of what my salary at South Carolina, what we had agreed on, was going to be, only that it was adequate for the time. For the sake of this anecdote let's just stipulate and say that it was $30,000, that I had accepted the offer of the dean for that sum.

"Well, I don't know, Jim. I'm not sure."

"Don't expect more than maybe fifteen or twenty. Don't let them think you are greedy. I'll work hard, behind the scenes, to try and get you as much as twenty. But I can't guarantee anything. Somewhere between fifteen and twenty. Maybe I can get you twenty if you're willing to take on an extra course."

Pause. What to say?

"Jim, I am deeply grateful for your interest and concern. And I look forward to working with you."

"If it all works out."

"Right. If it works out."

"I'll do my best for you."

"I know. And that's all I can ask for."

We finished the tea and I stood up to leave.

"One thing more," he said.

He was standing, too, and waved his hand inclusively indicating the whole neighborhood, the pleasant houses built around the lake, and maybe the whole of greater Columbia.

"This is a nice quiet neighborhood. With lots of nice people—doctors, lawyers, stock brokers, dentists and the like. A psychiatrist used to own this house of mine. Nice people live around here."

"I can see that."

"So, George, I hope you don't plan to invite a whole lot of your wild and wooly buddies to come on down here and visit. If you do they'll hop on some kind of a damn psychedelic bus and come and raise hell. And they will all want to come out here and see me. And that could be an embarrassment."

"Who do you have in mind?"

"You know—Dillard and Henry Taylor, Jim Seay, Peter Taylor, too. And Wilbur . . . people like that."

"Wilbur?"

"Yeah. He was on the phone to me for an hour and a half last night. He was all upset. He said to me, 'Jimbo, old buddy, tell me where I went wrong!'"

"No kidding?"

"It's really sad. I mean, between him and people like Updike and Cheever, calling up in the middle of the night and asking me for advice and comfort, I'm not getting enough sleep. The thing is, all kinds of people depend on me. I have to do the best I can for others. It goes with the territory, as they say."

⊷══◯══⊷

"Both Bruce Chatwin and Hemingway were 'mythomanes'," said Martha Gellhorn. *"They were not conscious liars. They invent to increase everything about themselves and their lives and believe it. They believe everything they say."*
                                    —Nicholas Shakespeare, *Bruce Chatwin*

"I ran a launch," he would say, "out into the Gulf where the schooner from Cuba would bring the raw alcohol and bury it on a sand-spit and we'd dig it up and bring it back to the bootlegger and his mother—she was an Italian, she was a nice little old lady, and she was the expert, she would turn it into Scotch with a little creosote, and bourbon." Neither Jack Falkner nor Bill Spratling believed these tales.

—Joseph Blotner, *Faulkner*

Pota's reputation for humor was well-earned, in his writing and in social discourse, and it was known by his friends that he could weave the most elaborate falsehoods with the most trustworthy of faces for as long as his listeners remained credulous.

—Joseph Heller, *Portrait of an Artist, as an Old Man*

Long before the death of James Dickey (January 19, 1997) there was a serious and busy little industry of Dickey scholarship and criticism. Beginning, more or less, with James Elledge's *James Dickey: A Bibliography 1947–1974* (Scarecrow Press), there was a wealth of ongoing studies. From 1984 on, there was the *James Dickey Newsletter* and many articles in literary, scholarly, and even popular commercial magazines. There were, first to last, a multitude of interviews, almost beyond counting, in all sorts of magazines and newspapers, on radio and television, on film. And there were the books, a surprising number. Among them: Laurence Lieberman, *The Achievement of James Dickey* (1968); Richard J. Calhoun (editor), *James Dickey: The Expansive Imagination* (1973); Richard J. Calhoun and Robert W. Hill, *James Dickey* (1983); Bruce Weigel and T. R. Hummer (editors), *The Imagination as Glory: The Poetry of James Dickey* (1984);

Ronald Baughman, *Understanding James Dickey* (1985); Neal Bowers, *James Dickey: The Poet as Pitchman* (1985); Harold Bloom (editor), *James Dickey: Modern Critical Views* (1987); Robert Kirschten, *James Dickey and the Gentle Ecstasy of Earth* (1988); Gordon Van Ness, *Outbelieving Existence: The Measured Motion of James Dickey* (1992); Ernest Suarez, *James Dickey and the Politics of Canon* (1993); Robert Kirschten (editor), *Critical Essays on James Dickey,* (1994); Kirschten, *"Struggling for Wings": The Art of James Dickey* (1977). And this list is incomplete. I have not, for example, mentioned books that include some writing about Dickey and his work, among other things. Books like Rosemary Daniell's *Fatal Flowers* (1980), which details a love affair they had.

In any case, while he was still alive, Dickey was the subject of an extraordinary amount of public critical (and personal) interest. Of all the books listed above, only Neal Bowers's *Poet as Pitchman* is less than uniformly adulatory and even Bowers assumes the value and importance of Dickey's finest work. Thus it can be argued, with the strength of strong evidence, that a goodly number of academics and critics had acquired a vested interest in the reputation of James Dickey well before his death.

Following his death there was what appears to be a well-orchestrated sequence of scholarly and biographical material, all part of the context of the publication of Henry Hart's full-scale biography. In 1998, Dickey's eldest son, Christopher, a journalist and novelist, published *Summer of Deliverance: A Memoir of Father and Son.* This often moving account of the relationship of father and son surprised and shocked many reviewers and readers with its loving but unsparing portrait of Dickey, simultaneously preparing the way for Henry Hart's biography even as it served to mute and undercut some of the negative and unpleasant information about Dickey. *Summer of Deliverance* was widely reviewed and (mostly) highly praised. Also in 1998 came *James Dickey: The Selected Poems*, edited by Kirschten. An odd, and oddly embarrassing little book is Mary Cantwell's *Speaking with Strangers* (1998), joining the others in preparing the way for the biography. Cantwell's book is a personal memoir concerning her failed marriage, her family, her travels, her editorial work for *Mademoiselle* magazine, and a long affair she had with the late James Dickey here known as "the balding man," whose first words to her at their cute meeting are vintage Dickey—"Mary, you evah been screwed till ya screamed?" In her account the relationship turned out to be a little different from her first impression and from Dickey's public persona: "Age—he was about ten years older than I—and alcohol had taken its toll of the balding man, and although he was never impotent, lie was demanding. Neither the athlete his publicity claimed nor the sexual Goliath his reputation promised, he was more myth than male." Of course, this little book is not the only kiss-and-tell vision of Dickey as lover. A former student, Rosemary Daniell, wrote about him as "The Great Southern Poet" in *Fatal Flowers* (Holt, 1980): "Southern men, I was learning, meant Southern lies, especially lies about personal intention, martial status, genealogy, money, and achievement. Sentimentality, about himself, even his fantasies of himself, is the hallmark of the grass-roots Southern male mind."

The following year, 1999, witnessed even more flurrying activity. Biographer Henry Hart edited (and dedicated to Dickey's literary executor, Matthew J. Bruccoli), *The James Dickey Reader,* with well-chosen selections from Dickey's published and uncollected poems, his fiction and criticism, and a concise version of the biographical facts in Hart's "Introduction." *Crux: The Letters* of *James Dickey*, edited by Matthew J. Bruccoli and Judith S. Baughman, is a 575-page selection from Dickey's correspondence, roughly twenty percent of the letters available, according to Bruccoli, and offers up a kind of chronological account of the intellectual and literary life of Dickey from May 1943 to November 1996, in and through Dickey's own words as he wrote to friends and enemies (often hopelessly interchangeable). In his introduction, Bruccoli explains the guidelines he used in his selection of the letters: "The double rationale for selection was first to document the growth of a major writer . . . then, second to document the ways he fulfilled his genius and advanced his career. Jim was unabashedly a careerist. . . . He deliberately promoted and exaggerated his several reputations—genius, drinker, woodsman, athlete—until the legends took over after *Deliverance*." Reviewers, taking their cue, probably from *The New York Times'* Michiko Kakutani, professed to be shocked by the self-portrait of a literary careerist that is limned in these letters. Here is Michiko cranking up: "Although there are a handful of passages in this volume that help illuminate Dickey's own work and attest to his love of books, a distressingly large portion is devoted to poetic politics: to snide put-downs of other poets, insider talk about prizes and fellowships and catty remarks about rival cliques and claques." This is more than a little disingenuous, though *Crux* and Hart's biography do show that a lot of Dickey's time and energy went into literary hustling and literary politics. He certainly schemed and scammed, tried to get awards and prizes, fellowships and grants, jobs and sinecures and honorary degrees. To achieve his worldly goals he appears to have been cheerfully willing to flatter and praise anybody who could conceivably help him at the moment, to injure others who might stand in his way, to betray any friend or ally, and to honor any enemy if that would help. He shows amazing lack of discrimination— why, for example, does he bother to flatter and try to charm much younger poets who would not be able to do much good or ill for him, one way or the other? In the case of Dave Smith, as with many others, it depends on what letter you read. Dickey is reasonably polite and even slightly humble in a letter of January 29, 1994, where he is trying to revise the poem "Last Hours" to suit Smith and his *Southern Review.* Elsewhere, in a letter of Peter Balakian, poet teacher at Colgate, Dickey has a some-what different point of view: "*Puella* is controversial, and will be attacked plenty; I expect Helen Vendler will come down on it, for she wishes to put one of her chicks, Dave Smith, who is a kind of follower of mine and did his doctoral dissertation on my work, up at my expense, and of course there are always people like Robert Bly and Donald Hall, who would do anything on earth to get at me." Another letter, not from *Crux* but quoted by Hart in the biography, a letter to poet Richard Tillinghast accom-panying a blurb by Dickey for Tillinghast's *The Knife and Other Poems*, covers some of the same territory: "The only danger you run from such an endorsement is that people like Helen Vendler, who for some reason detests me, will write you off as a follower of mine. But since Dave Smith is also a follower of mine or has certainly been influenced to an almost unparalleled degree by my work, and since for some reason Ms. Vendler likes *him,* maybe you won't come in for dismissal by her, or even worse, for her always-wrong praise."

Reviewers of *Crux* have been appropriately hypocriti-cal, confirming Dickey's picture of the poetry world as a seething series of penny ante conspiracies while refusing to admit the obvious: that his way has become and is the way of the American poetry world. True, as these letters reveal, he was willing to say or do almost anything for the sake of advancing his career and, whenever possible, to frustrate the careers of his peers, friend and enemy alike. To those he considered his betters and, often exactly the same, those most likely to be able to do him favors and good turns, he could be overwhelmingly humble, shame-lessly obsequious. Certainly he cultivated allies with flattery and promises and, by the same token, attacked and betrayed those self-same friends and mentors once he believed he had no more practical use of and for them. In fairness, it seems clear that Dickey's attitude and behavior was less common in his generation than in the later (present) generation of American poets. Always pre-scient, he saw the handwriting on the wall. His literary ways and means, unabashed and shameless to be sure, were executed with more style, bravado, and *chutzpah* than the next generation can seem to muster. And—sad truth must be known and acknowledged—there is no amount of flattery and chicanery, blatant or subtle, that can satisfy the hunger of too many American poets for honor and recognition. Dickey saw this and understood the game. Bruccoli makes a strong case in his introduc-tion to *Crux*: "He had a clear understanding of the odds against any poet, no matter how gifted, and he recognized that his poetry did not exist if it was not read."

Another kind of book, *James Dickey: Dictionary of Literary Biography: Documentary Series Volume 19* (1999), edited by Judith S. Baughman, serves to bring together a great deal of critical and referential material in a large scale study of Dickey's life and career, replete with photographs, rich with illustrative manuscript materials, drafts, and notes. Under the title "Teacher: James Dickey," the editor has assembled a gathering of previously unpublished class and lecture notes from his teaching days at the University of South Carolina.

Though he couldn't help himself from playing favorites with some students, nursing grudges against others, Jim earned a good reputation as a teacher.

On the job, on campus, we didn't see all that much of each other. Sometimes in the parking lot next to the English building. Sometimes going up on the elevator. . . .

It was there, on the lazy elevator, that the hat event took place. Both of us showed up and stepped aboard the elevator wearing broad-brimmed hats, cowboy hats. Jim's was his sheriff's hat from *Deliverance*. Mine was an elegant, supple, and heavy leather hat made for me by the Maiolo brothers. There were no girls or ladies on the elevator, so we didn't remove them. He looked at me and I looked at him. Nobody blinked. Then we arrived at our floor. The lackadaisical elevator doors began their slow-motion opening and closing. Jim stepped out. I followed. He turned toward me. "Don't misunderstand me, George, but the way I feel is there should only be one cowboy hat in this department. And I was here first."

Another time we were riding up or down—I forget— and the elevator was full of students going and coming to and from classes. When we stepped on the elevator, one of the students in the back looked at Jim and reacted. Nudging his companion. "Hey," he whispered audibly. "Look at that. Know who that is?" Jim nudged me and winked. "That's the guy that played the sheriff in *Deliverance*." The elevator stopped and we were pushed out by the tide of students. "Wait a minute! Wait just a big minute," Jim was calling to everybody, nobody in particular. "There's a whole lot more to me than just that."

Sometimes, irregularly enough to be unexpected, he would bang on my office door and then charge in. Once he came, red-faced and waving the local paper. The lead headlined story was about the murder of Sharon Tate and the others in Hollywood. We didn't know about Charley Manson yet. Just that this terrible murder had taken place. Jim mopped sweat with a pocket handkerchief and rattled the newspaper. "You know what this means, don't you, George? You know what this means?" Myself ever the straight man: "No, Jim what does it mean?"

"It means we're next. They are killing celebrities and we're next." He said he was going right out to buy an expensive and complex alarm and security system. He urged me to come with him and buy one, too.

"Thanks for thinking of me," I said. "But I don't think I'm really in as much danger as you are."

"You're probably right."

Another time he came in very quietly and felt for, found, and seated himself in a chair facing me. He seemed a little weak-kneed and pale.

"Anything wrong, Jim?"

"You better believe it, buddy. I feel just terrible."

"What's wrong?"

"Well . . . I just heard today that several people died over the weekend trying to white-water canoe on the Chattooga River."

"That's too bad."

"Don't you see, George? Don't you get it?"

"Get what?"

"I am directly and personally responsible for their deaths. I mean it. They either read *Deliverance* or saw the movie, and they got the idea to try it out themselves. And now they're dead and it's all my fault."

"I don't quite see it that way, Jim."

He wasn't listening. He groaned and stretched his long legs.

"Dumb bastards, they jump in a canoe—probably never even been in one in their lives—and paddle out to white water and *tump* over and drown on me. Before this is all over and done with I'll probably be responsible for the deaths of hundreds of people."

This was about a year or two after *Deliverance* (the film).

"Maybe you could put a warning sign alongside the river. *STAY OFF OF THIS HERE RIVER OR DIE!* And sign it James Dickey."

"This is not funny, goddamn it," he said. "Not funny at all."

"Well, Jim," I said, stealing a favorite line of his— what Lewis Payne, of Booth's Lincoln plot, said to the hangman—"you know best."

⤙═◎═⤚

Some things need to be said about Henry Hart's particular problems and solutions in writing the Dickey biography. First, there is the obvious fact that Hart's biography is not an "authorized" or "official" biography; and second, except for correcting a great many factual details and at the same time establishing a foundation for accurate information, it is not, because it cannot be, a "definitive" biography. The result of intense and difficult research, hundreds of personal interviews, and years of effort, it was and is a *necessary* biography. Neither is it an "unauthorized" biography of the kind developed and refined in a number of excellent studies by Carl Rollyson.

Rollyson deliberately and successfully aims to create a thorough and accurate literary biography without dealing with the complicated arrangements and permissions uniformly required by living authors or the estates of the dead, using instead the available public materials that can be found and effectively used by anyone willing and able to do the hard work. Hart's *James Dickey: The World as a Lie* is somewhere in between these extremes. Which, while not officially authorizing it, indeed professing that he did not want a biography of himself written, Dickey supported Hart's labor in a number of ways, asking and allowing his friends and kinfolk to cooperate with Hart and by permitting Hart to interview him in detail. We learn that the subtitle of Hart's book was Dickey's idea.

Hart lacked the security, limited as that may be, of a fully authorized biographer. He was, from first to last, in the unenviable position of having to satisfy the literary executor and the estate, both in general and in detail, or risk losing permission to quote much from Dickey's published works or from his letters and papers. Also, like almost any writer of anything in our day and age, Hart was required to satisfy the nervous legal worries of the publisher and its lawyers, made all the more onerous by the contemporary legal custom of preferring, under almost any set of circumstances, a compromise settlement to the risky drama of courtroom litigation regardless of the merits of a given case. A day in court is exactly what publishers' lawyers do not want. Hart's book was evidently delayed some time due to demands for changes of one kind or another. Of course this is the usual situation for most contemporary biographers, a condition that at once shapes and limits contemporary literary biography. Secondly, as noted, Hart's work was made more complicated by the other books that had recently appeared before he finished and published his own. It should be observed that these earlier books, especially *Summer of Deliverance* and *Crux*, though they aimed for honesty, were also intended to present a best-case point of view or, at least, not a worst-case scenario. As indicated, even though they "shocked" some reviewers, they also softened and muted the impact of Hart's biography, certainly reducing the element of surprise. But Hart's most serious problem was that Dickey, one of the most often interviewed and monitored writers in American literary history, hardly ever told anybody the truth about anything. He lied about everything even when there was no reason not to tell the truth. There is a certain amount of fun in seeing Dickey get away with this. Again and again, a five-minute phone call, a trip of about equal duration to any reference library, would have easily revealed the lie. But the press, including the literary press and, at its upper level, literary criticism, is deeply lazy and also, finally, shares Dickey's lack of interest in the tyranny of fact. Literary journalists, perhaps justly, are more interested in a good colorful story than in prosaic truth. From the beginning, Dickey understood the expectations of the press and lived up to them.

All well and good except, for Henry Hart, there was the Herculean labor of having to go back to square one and, like all the king's horses and all the king's men, to try to put the shattered facts back together again. This necessity meant, among other things, that it would have to be a very large, long biography (811 pages). Either that or ignore factual accuracy and hope for the best. I find myself wondering if Jim didn't want it that way—that the first real biography to be published, where much that had been concealed is now revealed and much that is false is corrected, is faulted for its steady focus on many small details rather than its large generalizations and its bold judgmental attitudes. Hart's story is only minimally judgmental—disillusioned maybe, yet always admiring the art and the artist at their best. But because almost every conceivable fact about Dickey's life turned out to be fiction, the biography became what it had to be—a long haul for the biographer and the reader. Other biographers will be along. Some are already waiting in the wings. And every one of them will have to depend on the hard and comprehensive labor of Henry Hart to get their easier task done.

Another problem the biographer faced is closely related. True and false alike, Dickey is the subject of many stories told by others. Clearly he did things to be noticed and remembered. For example, even his public poetry readings, apparently spontaneous in their ad libs and asides, in "mistakes" and in sudden inspiration, prove to have been tightly scripted. Speaking of which, one of Dickey's large lies escapes even Hart's skeptical safety net. Dickey called his intense schedule of poetry readings "Barnstorming for Poetry," asserting, and being taken at face value, that he did his readings not for gain and glory but to open up that "market" for poetry readings and his fellow poets. In fact, his extraordinary high fees wiped out the budgets of many institutions large and small and, if anything, had a counterproductive effect on future poetry readings. Robert Frost and, later, Dylan Thomas did some real "barnstorming for poetry." The combination of Dickey's exorbitant fees and rowdy behavior made it more difficult for other poets to follow after him. One might imagine that the next major difficulty Hart had to deal with in creating a coherent biography is a strength rather than a weakness. A lot of people knew James Dickey fairly well. There are many men and women who were witnesses to events in his life—hundreds of eyewitnesses, then. Over eight years Hart interviewed a great many of these people, family and friends, rivals and enemies, discovering inevitably that, like all eyewitnesses, their visions are highly subjective, often contradictory, and changed and modified by memory. This is a problem for all contemporary biographers, literary or otherwise. I believe Dickey was fully aware of this. Literary biography was a subject of great interest to him. He safely camouflaged himself in the diverse memories of a multitude of acquaintances. His actions generated a rich mythology of stories, apocryphal as well as authentic. And these stories have a life of their own like all gossip and oral history. Hart doesn't always get these mythological tales "right." But what is "right" and "wrong" in a myth?

⤙═◦═⤚

Quoting oneself is less than admirable but, in this instance, seems appropriate. Following the Hollins Conference in Creative Writing and Cinema, we put together a book of interviews with some of the writers who were there, including James Dickey. At first we were going to use photographs of each writer in the book, but the publisher refused to do that. So I wrote a short (less than a typed page) "snapshot" for each writer. Here is the snapshot of James Dickey from *The Writer's Voice* (1973):

> Legends, myths, fables and fabliaux, anecdotes, quotations from, hard and funny sayings, true and false, wheel and flock about him, a shrill invisible halo of birds explosively circling the edges of his wide-brimmed Warner Brothers sheriff's hat, the one he probably sleeps in (they say). No, not once upon a time an ad man for nothing at all, and he can do some splendid impersonations, best of all (I think) King

Kong and Marlon Brando. Yes, more masks and costumes than a whole Halloween party, more hidden rabbits and aces than a magician. Something else! But . . . but behind all obvious shucks and colorful charades is the powerful dedicated poet and a complex man burning alive in pure intensity. Not even his big, strong, long-legged body can deny his curious gentleness, his clear vulnerability. His head-high easy swagger does not disguise his suffering. Jim can be like a carnival pitchman because the truth is so precious to him and always so threatened. To know him, the only way, look for him, truly tall and strong and all alive, in his poems.

Novelist, and former student of Dickey and myself, Ben Greer, called me from Columbia to report that on an impulse he drove out to Dickey's old address at Lake Katherine. He had heard that the house had been sold. Wanted to see it one more time before somebody else moved in. He drove out there and was startled to discover that the house was gone. Not just knocked down, but vanished without a trace.

"There is no sign that there ever was a house there," he told me.

"The house has been completely destroyed and removed. The land has been planted with trees and shrubs. It looked like a little park. I got down on my hands and knees and crawled around looking for any-thing—a nail, a screw, a piece of plaster or broken glass, anything at all to prove the house had been there. I couldn't find a thing. It was really weird."

It is weird to hear about that, too. No sign or indication of the good times and the bad times there. Many a story, much laughter, a lot of good whiskey. Thanks to Jim we had a lot of fun once upon a time.

It was there, during or right after the shooting of the

Deliverance movie, that John Boorman told the Lee Marvin story. (It might have been Boorman who told it. That's how I remember it. But it could just as well have been Jim, himself, repeating and embellishing it. No matter who told it, it was Boorman's story, as told in that house.)

Before *Deliverance* Boorman had directed an odd little picture called *Hell in the Pacific*. It had only two actors in it—Lee Marvin and the great Japanese actor, Toshiro Mifune. The plot line, as I recall, was that these two old-timers, leftovers from World War II, share an island where they spend most of their time hunting each other with intent to kill. One day a huge hurricane comes along, and in order to escape to another uninhabited island, they have to cooperate. Working together, they manage the escape. And then . . . they start right in with the hunt to kill routine. The end.

When this low-budget film premiered in Hollywood, it was a pretty small, quiet affair. Mifune wasn't about to fly over from Japan. Mr. and Mrs. Boorman hopped into their Volkswagen van and picked up Lee Marvin and went to see the movie in the middle of the afternoon. A few little old ladies in tennis shoes applauded their arrival and departure. When the film was over, the cast party wasn't a big problem: "Hey, Lee, where would you like to go to supper?"

Marvin allowed that he would like to go out to Venice, by the beach, and get really drunk and eat a greasy steak.

They found themselves in a bar that Marvin liked, trying to keep up with him, more or less, drink for drink. Soon the Boormans were pouring most of their drinks under the table and Marvin was having a good time. At 2:00 a.m. the bar closed and everybody stumbled out to the street. When they approached the van, the Boormans were astonished that Lee Marvin climbed up on top and settled down, prone, on the luggage rack. He wouldn't answer them and wouldn't come down. They discussed the situation. Marvin lived up the coast about thirty minutes drive from Venice on the freeway. They decided to drive very, very slowly in the breakdown lane on the almost empty highway (it was now three o'clock in the morning).

Everything went along fine. After about an hour, at ten miles an hour, they suddenly found themselves being pulled over by the California Highway Patrol, colored lights blinking. Boorman stopped and waited. The patrolman got out of his car, walked back and rapped on the window on the driver's side. Boorman rolled down the window. The patrolman saluted.

"Excuse me, sir," be said. "But do you realize you have Lee Marvin on top of your car?"

Only in Hollywood. As they say.

There is an anticlimactic ending. The police assembled a posse of police cars, rather like those years later in the O. J. chase, and convoyed the Boormans and Lee Marvin, still obstinately clinging to the luggage rack, to Marvin's house. Where they were able to coax him down and into his bed.

Plenty of laughter and fresh drinks all around at Dickey's house.

Now all the words and even the echoes of them are long gone. Lost except for fragments of fading and changing memory. Not a rusty nail, not a sliver of broken glass. Nothing at all. Except, as it should be, the words of the dead poet in print, on audio tape, on the soundtrack of several films. And those words are as fresh and clear as when he wrote them and spoke them. And, as is the case with all true poetry, they will be perfectly new and shining for a new generation and a long time to come.

Good Medicine: Some Personal Notes on the Art and Life of Madison Jones

Every serious writer, however clearly aware of the impossible odds, would like to persuade the world of something.

—Madison Jones

I was brought up to believe that it was bad manners and, maybe even worse, an act of cowardice to attempt to camouflage one's own failures behind a screen of complaint and self-pity and the hypocrisies of lame apology. Nevertheless . . . nevertheless that is exactly what I have to do here: to allow that a great mass of long-committed work, at once seriously delayed and aggravated by an eye condition that is waiting its turn for surgery, has prevented me from doing the right thing, the thing I truly wanted to do. What I really wanted to do, the very least that this altogether appropriate celebration of the art of Madison Jones calls for, was to sit down and carefully reread that work in the chronological order that it appeared and to offer up some serious critical appreciation. I had read the books that way, beginning with *The Innocent* (1957) on up through *Last Things* (1989), as soon as they were published and available. And I had and have strong memories of them, of the great pleasure and green envy I felt when I first encountered them. All those stories, sentence by gracefully turned sentence, solidly

constructed, inhabited with interesting and fully dimensional characters, and characterized, in general and in
detail, by Jones's flinty, impeccable integrity, moved me
to admiration and taught me much—including some of
my own limitations.

I haven't known Madison Jones well or long (maybe
twenty years of acquaintanceship) in person, but I was
aware of his presence and his example for most of my
adult life. He has said somewhere that at times in his
youth he spent more time at athletics than at his studies.
So did I. Two of the several sports I participated in, with
clumsy enthusiasm if not with much natural grace or
ability, were track and swimming. And I recall, my
muscles recall, that in both those sports while one's
attention was always focused on the care and mainte-
nance and exploitation of one's own body, you also had
to be aware of and alert to what was happening all around
you. Art is not a foot race, thank the Lord, but the
metaphor has some truth to it. What I'm saying is that
from the beginning of my own professional career as a
writer I have been aware of Jones as somebody worthy
and well worth reading and knowing about.

At the beginning, beyond the work itself, all that I
knew was secondhand, hearsay and gossip. I knew that he
had been associated with Vanderbilt, and I took him to be
the fair-haired principal fiction writer (as his contemporary, James Dickey, was the fair-haired principal poet) of
the ongoing Vanderbilt-Agrarian-Fugitive crowd, few of
whom I knew or knew very much about at the time. This
vague supposition, identity by association, as it were, was
confirmed for a time when I first read Walter Sullivan's
"The Continuing Renascence: Southern Fiction in the
Fifties" (published in *South: Modern Southern Literature in
its Cultural Setting*, edited by Louis D. Rubin, Jr. and

Robert D. Jacobs, 1961). *The Innocent* was brand new then, and I found myself nodding in agreement with Sullivan on point after point as he praised the work: "The novel is amazingly ambitious. Image is piled on image in what seems to be an effort to encompass totally the various conflicts and tensions that surround Duncan Welsh [the protagonist] in his rural Middle Tennessee world. Jones is superb in his handling of nature: there is probably no one writing today who can create woods and fields and animals and sky with as much feeling and accuracy and dramatic effectiveness." A point as true now, and in all his work, as then. "Jones's virtues are many and his faults are minor and few," Sullivan concluded.

To make my next point, I must turn to Walter Sullivan again. Here the reader should know that since then, and for a long time until now, I have been pleased to think of Walter Sullivan as my friend. I always respected the integrity and validity of his criticism, a fact that made his remarks about my first novel, *The Finished Man*, in the same "Southern Fiction in the Fifties" essay smart more than they might have: "Garrett's *The Finished Man* is in every particular such a poorly conceived, poorly written book that it does not deserve to be named in the company of the other novels discussed here. The characters are flat; the plot is stale; the pace is slow; the prose is at best pedestrian and at worst illiterate." (Wow! Enough stuff like that could hurt a fellow's feelings.) At that point, briefly to be sure, the innocent Madison Jones, author of *The Innocent*, became the enemy. Which made me all the more anxious to keep up with his work, to follow with interest his career as it unfolded. I may have wished catastrophe upon him and on the whole Vanderbilt crowd. I don't remember, but it seems likely. But not for long. What happens is that one's own work, good or ill, eats up all energy and dedication and there is nothing much left over for the sake of malice. Besides, anger has never served much as inspiration to me. I learned soon enough that anger is a crippling, self-defeating sin. I can still work up a half-decent rage about many trivial things, real and imaginary slights, for example, but even at the high moment of it, I am fully aware that it is not doing me any good at all. In any case, I didn't stay angry with Madison Jones or Walter Sullivan or the whole crew from Vanderbilt for very long. True, I couldn't resist the opportunity when it came along a couple of times to affect the authentic stance of a Low Country South Carolina snob for whom all upcountry people, especially from far, rude places like the hills and hollows of Tennessee, were hillbillies and ridge-runners, whose pretensions at intellectual significance were as ridiculous as their social accomplishments and aspirations. Lucky for me, nobody paid any attention.

Meanwhile I had an extra good reason ("Let's see what the enemy is up to.") to read, with care and growing, grudging admiration, the works of Madison Jones as they came along: *Forest of the Night* (1960), *A Buried Land* (1963), *An Exile* (1967), *A Cry of Absence* (1971), *Passage Through Gehenna* (1978), *Season of the Strangler* (1982), and *Last Things* (1989). Both of us have, in the requisite contemporary fashion, moved from publisher to publisher. We were both at Doubleday when *Season of the Strangler* was published, and I heard a good deal from editors there expressing their enthusiasm for Jones and his work.

Truth is, there was yet another turning point, a point at which all sense of rivalry and/or petty, injured pride fell away. While I was teaching at Princeton in the 1970s, one of my students was Madison Smartt Bell, a brilliant student and brilliantly gifted, whose outspoken admiration for the fiction of Madison Jones stirred up my own excitement, opened up new ways (for me) to think about it and sent me back to the books.

Lately, waiting for the new book to come along, I have stumbled on something quite wonderful, which I strongly commend to one and all who share an appreciative interest in the works of Madison Jones. Chances are that some readers have missed it. Jones's essay for the series *Contemporary Authors Autobiography Series* (Volume 11, 1990, pp. 171–187) is graceful in form and content, fascinating in what he has chosen to tell us about his life and especially in the straightforward account of the making of his books.

From the life, I learn that we have more in common than I realized. I learn that both of us have spent youthful, memorable times on family farms, he at Sycamore Farm, outside Nashville, "one of the last places where, when people stopped talking, silence would come down." I spent happy times at my grandfather's remote farm in North Carolina where I learned to milk and to plough (with horses and with mules), the ways and means of chickens, the picking of vegetables and wild berries, the hoot of an owl, the reedy cackle of a black caucus of crows. I learn that, just as we were pretty serious Episcopalian people (if that isn't an oxymoron), his Protestant Presbyterian faith was strong and strict: "Our Presbyterian religious training had real teeth in it." That we both left college twice, interrupting our formal education, myself from Princeton and he from Vanderbilt. That we both served in the U.S. Army overseas. That we both have had some of our best work rejected by publishers. I may have him beat on this. *The Innocent*, the book that he describes as "the one that came nearest to being autobiographical," was rejected three times before it found a home. *Death of the Fox* earned fifteen rejections before Doubleday took it. Both of us have been teachers of writing and literature for most of our adult lives to earn a living and to be free to write the things we want to and care about. He speaks for me, too, when he says "I took all my teaching seriously." Admitting to being "a sort of metaphysical apologist for the South," he also allows that "I still look with pain on the defeat we suffered in that war [The Civil War]." Doesn't everyone?

We have shared some of the same mentors. One of them is Monroe Spears. We both had *Sewanee Review* fellowships, his in fiction and mine in poetry. Though he was much closer than I ("Andrew Lytle is, I believe, the most remarkable man I have known."), we both were friends of the late Andrew Lytle.

At a deeper level we hold to some of the same fundamental assumptions. Madison Jones might be speaking for me when he writes: "Evil is a prime fact of our existence: we may be forgiven it but we cannot escape it." And his description of the flaws at the heart of modern secular America asks for and receives my whole-hearted agreement. "In the end," he writes, "the one shared absolute is the idea of equality, from which intellectual and moral relativism and finally cynicism derive."

A difference? I think I have always been (since the crib, probably) more cynical than Madison Jones, a condition that has done me no great injury, but surely limits my ability to write in unmixed forms. Comedy, be it ever so dark or grotesque, is always a shadow dancer in my work. Spared from cynicism, Jones can write, in

Monroe Spears's words about *A Cry of Absence*, "an authentic pure, and deeply moving tragedy."

Finally, another thing. Madison Jones and I are both members, and glad of it, of the Fellowship of Southern Writers, whose chief function is to recognize and reward, with a series of prizes, younger and newer Southern writers who deserve recognition and reward. It is meet and right, by the same token, that the body of work, of *art*, so far created by Madison Jones should be here recognized and rewarded with serious attention. Even if this brief piece falls far short of what I wanted, my bounden duty, to do, I am happy to be here, honored to be included among others who honor him and his work.

William Goyen:
Brother to Anyone with Ears to Hear

In fact and in flesh, *in person* as they say, we did not know each other much or well. We had worked together at a couple of writers' conferences and had met socially a few times. I remember once, to my surprise and delight, he showed up, just there, sitting in the small audience, at a poetry reading I gave one evening at Cooper Union in New York City. I didn't even know he was in town at the time. To show up at a poetry reading, even a friend's, when you don't have to and the friend won't be any the wiser, is way above and beyond the call of duty.

I remember what he looked like, of course, in photographs and in fact—tall, slender, but sturdy, well-formed, handsome, and by the time I actually met him, wonderfully weather-beaten—an honest and honorable East Texas face. I remember more acutely his tact and compassion, his good humor and his real skill with people. That last surprised me. I remember once seeing him act (skillfully) as toastmaster at a banquet in Houston. He was an adept, sophisticated, yes, *clever* toastmaster. I was much impressed. He told jokes, presented awards, and made everyone feel good.

Occasionally we did each other routine professional favors. For example, when I had to leave Princeton for a semester, I suggested and recommended Bill as my replacement. And he got the job. I recommended him also to the people at Hollins College (where he already had such dedicated fans as Richard Dillard and Allen Wier) as a writer-in-residence; and recommended to him that he should go. He went there and was wonderful and was much loved.

So, inevitably, we shared some students over the years—Madison Smartt Bell was one of them from Princeton days. And we shared some close friends. We even shared (as friend) an editor, Sam Vaughan at Doubleday, and sometimes communicated through him.

Near the end of his life—though I had no way to know how near the end was and, indeed, was under a kind of hearsay impression that his health was much improved—Bill did me an enormous favor. He agreed, without reluctance, to read all the way through the huge and unwieldy manuscript of my novel, *The Succession*, about which I was plagued with more than my usual quota of questions and doubts. He took precious time to read it with care and to write a response to me. Matter of fact he wrote me a couple of letters as he went along, letters that lifted my flagging spirits and greatly encouraged me. Later, as a practical matter, he called and dictated a blurb for the book to Sam Vaughan.

I am ashamed now, of course, to have stolen that time and energy from him. But, nevertheless, I am happy for his attention and shall always be grateful for it.

I shall always be grateful to him for more than that, far more—for his art and his example as an artist. I came to *The House of Breath* just about the time it came out, a time when, after fooling around with writing all my life, as long as I could remember, I was finally committed (without having a clue what that commitment might mean) to the art of writing as my vocation and my life. I can't even begin, not in a few words here and maybe not in many, to tell what that book meant to me. I had just returned from a job in East Texas, all over East Texas as a matter of fact, knew something about the "reality" of which he wrote, just as, with some blood kin there, I knew something about the people, too. But the book was a profound influence. Not an influence in the conventional sense. I never even imagined myself writing *like* William Goyen. From the first he was wholly admirable and wholly inimitable. But in an almost absolute sense both his achievement, then and there and in the other, later works as they came along one by one, and his example—the example of his grace in survival as an artist of dedication and integrity, his *courage*, in good times and bad, courage that would be sorely tested and would finally triumph over fact and flesh—all these things were for me like trail signs blazed by a genuine and adventurous explorer. They were and are lights in and against the dark. In that deeper sense he dares (almost childishly, "I dare you," wonderfully so) anyone to try and follow after him—to aim to do the right thing with one's gifts and to try to do it well.

There is no dwindling or diminishment in his story. *Arcadio* has all the power and originality and the mystery that other works, early and late, make manifest. And these days I keep close by, and reckon I will do so while I live and I can, the printed version of his talk of 13 April 1983 at New York University—"Recovering: Writing and Healing." When I first read the words, I could hear him. When I read the words and heard him, he became, as I believe he intended to be, my brother. Not mine alone, but brother to anyone with ears to hear. A brother who will not permit the easy choices of despair and silence. At least not before the true time to embrace pure silence has arrived. He will not permit me (or you, either, if you listen) to succumb to the powerful temptation to deny the holy mystery of myself and thus of others.

True and False Confessions

Indulge Me a Little:
An Interview with George Garrett

BY MADISON SMARTT BELL

I just read an essay by Monroe Spears that says that your two historical novels, Death of the Fox *and* The Succession, *take the form of the novel as far as it possibly can be taken, along with* Ulysses *and a couple of others he mentions. It looks that those two are going be fairly well established. I wanted to ask first how you got started on the period?*

I got started at Princeton doing a Junior Paper. I was working on the poetry of Sir Walter Ralegh. And at that time there was a fairly new text out in paperback by a woman named Agnes Latham. In the introduction, she got me really interested in him as a person. She pointed out that there hadn't been a biography of him for many, many years. I said, "Oh good, that is something I can do. I will be the one to do that."

I didn't realize it, but by the time it gets into the introduction of a paperback, anyone who is going to be doing it is doing it already. But in a vague way I started reading about Ralegh, keeping little notes, thinking I would do a biography. I continued to do this until I went in the service where it was no longer possible, but I didn't really forget about it. Came back, and by that time there were plenty of biographies on the market and there have been ever since.

So I realized that I couldn't do any real biography, but it had been enough to interest me a whole lot and I continued to study it and fool around with it. There never was any book for a long time, just various attempts at one thing and another. You could tell I was working on it, but I didn't know what I was working on.

Then you published several other books in the meantime. Why did Death of the Fox *take so long to write?*

Partly because I was doing all these other things at the same time. I worked in Hollywood. All kind of teaching and publishing, all kinds of other stuff. And I just never knew enough to be able to do it. I didn't know what I was looking for. And during the period that I was trying to write that book there was the great explosion of Elizabethan scholarship. As fast as I would think I was reading everything I should know, fifty more books would come out.

There was a point when I could have just given up on the book and spent the rest of my life trying to keep up with all the books that were being done about the subject. It was virtually impossible to know enough to feel at ease writing about past time. I finally just kind of gave out. I was locked into it by that time. That was going to be it. I just had to go and write.

You ended up knowing a hell of a lot. Were you trying to research particular topics or gobbling up everything?

It was more like gobbling up everything because I didn't know what I was looking for. I read as many lives of Ralegh as I could, but that was just the beginning. The other kind of research would follow a topic for a while and that would lead to something else. Trying to know enough to do it, handling truckloads of notes, kind of got in my way. It may have been that they were so disorganized. Maybe it would have been different if computers were around. So, anyway I found I couldn't really do it that way. I would look up all the notes I had on castles or something—

—and it would drive you crazy—

—drive me crazy and I wouldn't get any writing done. So, I changed the model of the book from term paper to test. Which are the only two models we have when we come out of college: you write a paper or a test. So I changed it over to test and then I just closed the trunk and wrote it off the top of my head.

Now here is the bad part. The down side is, just like with any other test you cram for, that you forget. Two weeks after *Death of the Fox* was published I couldn't remember Ralegh's middle name if he had one, let alone any details. So when I came to do *The Succession*, which had been planned, I didn't know what it was going to be like but I thought it would be real easy because I knew everything. I opened up the blank sheet of paper and I didn't know anything! And I had to start over and do the same thing, exactly, back to square one.

The Ralegh in Death of the Fox, *is that a portrait of the real Ralegh, do you think, or an invention, or both?*

It has got to be a little of both and it has got to be somewhat distorted. Even unintentionally distorted. Things are in there because I remembered them at a particular time. Right? In other words, it partakes of the peculiar urgency of memory.

You never cheated at all?

Basically not. It was like an open book exam, but you've got time as a factor. So, what I think is that insofar as the book has any singular living quality, it is the quality of being really remembered. Okay. It is really remembered, because I am straining my memory trying to recall what I read about Sir Walter Ralegh. The urgency of my memory gets in there. That gives it a certain kind of excitement it might not have had otherwise. On the other hand, the risk of that kind of arrangement is that you will forget. And I frankly forgot some of the major events in his life, some of which contradict or greatly modify positions I did take about it. I thought, "So what, let them worry about it. I would be cheating if I did." And I didn't mind the figure that emerged. So it is quite true that he is a distorted figure and certain amounts of historical fact and detail about him seem to have been suppressed. But they were not really suppressed, they were forgotten.

Yet it seems to be completely exhaustive in the way that it reads.

I don't know what real experts on Ralegh would think. There were a few notices that said, "Wonder why he didn't mention his ten-year obsession with so-and-so. . . ." Either I had never heard of it or I had forgotten it. That didn't worry me so much as long as I got the basic outline of his life. And it was a slight cheat to have him in the process of remembering as I am trying to remember. To put the whole story at the end of his life so he is allowed to forget aspects of his own career.

*It's a twenty-four-hour novel covering at least a hundred years
of history. How did you arrive at the strategy of treating periods
of his life in terms of profession?*

I was trying to figure out a way to deal with his life,
historically, and when he was on the scaffold he said this:
"I have been a soldier, a courtier, and a sea-faring man.
And the temptations of the least of these are able to
overthrow a good mind and a good man." So I thought,
"Terrific. I will just treat him in those capacities."

Sometimes you make a choice that is almost totally
whimsical, but you are grasping for some kind of frame,
and then if it seems to work you will live with it. It is not
inevitable at all.

*One of the things in both of the books is a sharp analysis of
political behavior. What do you think, was their political life
like ours or not?*

I think in many ways it was. It had more integrity in a
certain way—you died for your positions. You don't die
for them now, you just deny everything alleged and run
on the other ticket. I think you would shake a lot of guys
out of American politics like rotten apples off a tree if
they thought their lives were on the line. Other than that
it was very similar, except that you lost your head instead
of your office.

There is a lot of detail, especially in The Succession, *about
ordinary people, rather than historical personalities. Do you
think you ended up knowing what the basic life of the time was
like?*

I'm not sure that I did. What one ends up with in a work of fiction of that kind, ideally, is a capacity to imagine living at that time with the elements that you have been given.

Living as yourself?

That is about the most that you can figure. The deeper I got into it the more alien it seemed. I never really got around that. I still think that is the main impact.

They weren't much like us, then.

No. That began to be one of the points to make in *Death of the Fox* and more strongly in *The Succession*. The more you knew about them the odder they appeared, by our standards. Then it gets really quite startling if you realize that it hasn't been all that long ago—human beings have changed that much in such a short time. They can't even perceive the world in the same way.

Does this sort of discovery cause you to believe in progress?

No.

What about progress of intellect and sensibility, evolution of that kind? Do you think it exists at all?

I have my doubts. Are you thinking of whether people are more intelligent or knowledgeable? They know different things. Certainly I don't think they are any better. That would be an outrageous argument for someone living in the twentieth century to make. But I am thinking one of the characteristics of the twentieth century is how often and how successfully we lie to ourselves. Just the other day I was listening to one of these pontificators—one of these guys with the deep voice on National Public Radio. Always has the perfectly rounded thing, like a little sonnet, about whatever the issue is. So the pontificator said, "We have come to value human life; it has more meaning than it might have had in earlier centuries." Oh, yeah? How many people were killed, eighty million total in World War II?

We value human life so much in the United States that we go to enormous lengths to let people off for murder, rape, arson, pillage, and looting—but the main statistical aim of all traffic control is to keep the number of deaths down to fifty thousand a year. If I told you that that was my goal in life: to hold down that number of deaths to fifty thousand a year, you would probably have the right to say that I was bullshitting you when I was talking about how you must preserve human life at all costs. It seems to me that we are much more duplicitous intellectually than anybody in our recent history, and that we deceive ourselves in millions of ways.

Another small example. Think about this as to whether it represents intellectual progress. Elizabeth could forbid discussion of certain topics. The topic of her succession was illegal to discuss in public. During particularly the last ten years of her life when it was a very important issue. Now, we are very proud of our complete freedom of discussion. Up to a point this is true. When, about two years ago, there was some serious debate about what our strategy should be in the event of a nuclear war, it was suggested quite seriously by a large number of publications run by some of the great liberal minds of America that we shouldn't be talking about this because it would lead people to think about a subject that is unthinkable. Their argument was that if you think about the unthinkable, it becomes more thinkable, and it is more likely to happen. Therefore, so that those dumb-dumbs out there won't start thinking about nuclear war, best we should never bring it up.

Okay. What's the difference? A serious argument could be made, and indeed was made in 1978 in the Harvard Commencement speech by Solzhenitsyn, which had people throwing beer cans at him (and brickbats, in the press). What he said very simply was that it is wonderful to be in a place where there is no state censorship. It would be even more wonderful if there wasn't such a mindset that prevented any new idea from ever surfacing. One of the great tragedies of a free society is when they use self-censorship to such an extent that they might as well have state censorship. There are any number of things that have become unthinkable to discuss. You would be instantly thrown out the room. And what is the difference between that and the Queen saying, "Goddammit, nobody talk about the succession. They will probably kill me off if they keep talking about it."

Who can deny some technological progress? But the Elizabethans did at least weigh the consequences of the technological progress they had available to them. There are cases where they changed their mind about something they were going to do because of the dangers involved.

In terms of making an advance in sophistication?

Yes. Old people in America, who were here when the very first automobiles appeared, have said that if they had ever imagined the filth and danger these damned machines would bring into their lives, they would have stamped them out then and there and we would be running around on horses. Now that to us is unthinkable—that someone could stamp out technological progress—but of course the Elizabethans did.

You mentioned cases?

They had a real problem about heating because they didn't have boilers and high tech. The obvious solution was that they had plenty of coal. And they did not have plenty of wood. What they told them was, "Quit clouding up the sky and fucking up everything, and until we find something else, do a lot more side-straddle hops and laps around the house." It is a little easier when you can tell people to be cold. "The Queen don't want you to burn none of that coal." Essentially it was easier because they had a dictatorial society, but they decided it wasn't worth the aggravation to get heavily into coal at that time. Well, a hundred years later, they didn't give a shit; they blacked out the sky of England and some of it has just gotten visible for the first time again within our lifetime, up there in the Midlands.

In the light of everything you've been saying, what is the meaning of history anymore? What do you get from it, if it is not really progressive?

If it is not progressive, it is not so much the meaning of it as the value of it that's in question. There are two sorts of possible notions about it. One of them would be that it is especially significant that things haven't changed that much; there is no particular movement in history—how people handled their problems in the past is much more relevant than we might have imagined. To approach it not as an inferior form of modern life but as a separate and distinct culture. When we approach the Elizabethans or the Romans or anybody else in the past, it should make the past very different for us, and much more pertinent. At least it changes the perspective for us so that we have different things to learn from it than how they were so stupid they couldn't invent television.

One of our assumptions about progress seems to be that each generation accumulates more knowledge than the past generation. That we are like giants—we are standing on the shoulders of the last generation like cheerleaders on top of a pyramid. The only problem with that is it seems that we forget as much at the other end as we are learning at this end. The sum total of knowledge does not increase, which is one of the things which makes it so difficult for us ever to have enough information to properly imagine the past.

I want to ask about the language of the novels, which is neither antiquarianly exact nor like any modern language that ever was. If you compare it to the actual letters of Elizabeth and James, which you use in The Succession, *it's similar in feeling but not exactly the same. How did you arrive at that style?*

Well, that of course was always going to be the big problem. By the second time around I knew that was going to be the major problem. The first time I stumbled over it and didn't try to deal with it. It would have been fun to do a totally antiquarian, exact thing, except it would have taken me thirty years to learn enough about the way they used language to be at ease with it and then it wouldn't have meant anything to anybody else who hadn't spent thirty years the same way. So I did something somewhat similar to what I described as the use of the facts of the past. I crammed my head for a long time, without trying to get specific, with phrases and things, reading all different kinds of Elizabethan prose, until I got whipped up like in a Waring blender. I tried to get the rhythmical sense and then I kind of reduced it into a modern equivalent. I wanted a language that was a little strange, that was clearly not the English that we hear, but wasn't incomprehensible. I didn't want to move in the direction of Bergman in *The Silence*. The uses of incomprehensibility—I didn't want that.

I've noticed in letters and things and in longhand draft of The Succession *that you write on those long yellow pads and in very big letters, about six lines to a legal-sized sheet. Have you always done that?*

No, not always. At certain points I tried to cram as much as I could on a page. I got interested in writing really, really small because I noticed that the manuscripts I saw by Faulkner, Eugene O'Neill, etc., were tiny, tiny and got a lot on a page. And I thought that is what you had to do to be a good writer. Practically putting scripture on the head of a pin. But once I started writing big it just got bigger and bigger. When I was doing *Death of the Fox* there was a woman here in Charlottesville, and from all over the country I would send her the manuscripts in longhand. She would type it and I would work from the typed version. My wife, Susan, typed the final version. But for the first draft I wanted to make sure that she didn't miss anything in my handwriting, so I wrote large for her to be able to read it very easily—these huge packages of yellow pads. I think it filled her garage.

Do you have that stuff anymore?

She said, "What shall I do with it?" one day. I said, "Burn it."

How many drafts did Death of the Fox *go through?*

I don't know. I honestly don't. I didn't keep track. I didn't say this is draft number one, this is draft number two. Everything was kind of ongoing at the same time. But I would be doing new stuff while I was revising old stuff. Sometimes I lost sections that I revised and would have to do it over again.

Is that story true about finding the same scene done twice from different points of view when you reread the 2,000 final pages?

I think that really happened. But I don't remember which one it is. The weirdest thing of that kind that ever happened to me was losing a short story. I thought I could make something else out of the same material, wrote the story again and then the first story was found. And comparing them, there were only about five words different. There was no intent to rewrite the first story. So the concentration at that point was like hypnosis.

That's amazing. How many drafts did the first three novels go through?

It's hard, because of the way I was working, to really call something a draft. I wrote *The Finished Man* in Rome when I was over there in 1958. And what I would do is every day start out at the beginning and rework up to as far as I had gone and then write some new stuff.

That's what you'd do in the morning?

Yes.

So, when you get halfway through, it gets to be a long morning.

It does. It's kind of silly. I finally figured that out after doing it. But I read that Hemingway did it, so I thought that it must be the way to do it. But the effect of it is that the first few chapters get revised daily, whereas for the last part, by the time you get there, however much revision you do, you are actually doing one draft.

Starting into the first novel, did you have particular influences? Did you see yourself in relation to the Agrarians or the Fugitives or Southern Renaissance writers at all?

Not really, but I had certainly read them—and had read an awful lot of Faulkner. I was trying not to do something that sounded like everything they did, but inevitably some of my concerns were the same concerns.

What about Faulkner as an influence?

I went the opposite direction from some I know. Example: Reynolds Price says somewhere that he is almost completely unfamiliar with Faulkner. Very early he read one book or something and decided he didn't want to read any more because he just didn't want to be influenced. I did the opposite; I read it all. I think you have to do one or the other. I wanted to use the things he had taught us but I didn't want to sound like him, to pick the rhythms and the words and the tropes and devices. In the best sense, there are ways to use the influence and work better. That's what I wanted to do, and whether it was always successful or not, I don't know.

As for the others I did indeed read a great many. Southern novelists interested me the most. Warren, Lytle. I like Tate. Caroline Gordon. I was tremendously excited by reading the first things of Carson McCullers. I didn't know Flannery O'Connor until a little bit late when I began to get stories turned down: "I like this story a lot and I would publish it but it sounds too much like Flannery O'Connor." I had Flannery O'Connor mixed up with Flann O'Brien. Anybody named Flannery. I just thought it was some guy from Ireland. It bugged me because I hardly could have been influenced by somebody I never heard of and thought was an Irishman. So I was greatly pleased, years later, to find in her book of letters one that says: "Katherine Anne Porter came through town. We had lunch. She tells me I write a lot like George Garrett. Who is he? I hope he's no one terrible." So I was really pleased that she had had the same dilemma.

The Finished Man is a political novel, and I'm wondering how you'd compare Southern politics with the politics of Elizabethan England.

In Southern politics failure didn't cost you your life then either, but there weren't too many second chances. As late as the forties and early fifties, you get aced in Southern politics and you are finished. Except, strangely enough, for Claude Pepper, who's the model for the Senator in that novel. He was one of the leading Democratic Senators, very likely would have been Vice President instead of Lyndon Johnson. Instead he got beaten out of the Senate by his own protégé. The book is modeled closely enough on the Pepper/Smathers race that most of the papers down Southeast reviewed it with pictures of them and discussed it in that way.

Anyway, Claude Pepper survived all of this. A few years went by and he found himself—he is now a major national figure again: Claude Pepper the Congressman, now eighty-some years old, leading the aged people of America. They don't even remember Claude Pepper the Senator.

There is a story that goes with this. Susan and I both worked for Jack Kennedy, years and years ago. My job was to try to talk writers into voting for Kennedy. And I must tell you that I made endless phone calls and many famous writers of my generation (I can remember their names and I hope they're reading this interview) said, "Kennedy and Nixon, Kennedy and Nixon—two of a kind, I'm not voting!" Later, many of these same guys were very passionate about marching against the Vietnam War. But after they made that statement I didn't take their judgment about Vietnam or anything else very seriously. I thought they were assholes and that their knowledge of politics was zero, and I am not progressively oriented enough to think that they acquired more knowledge as they went along.

Anyway, very shortly after Kennedy's election, I was invited to a Kennedy party and got introduced to one of his hotshot guys as somebody from Florida. This guy said, "Tell me how we can win over and get next to the Democrats in Florida. We didn't do well there in the election." Pepper had come into Congress that same election, so I told him, "Go talk to Claude Pepper. He's a winner." And the guy said, "I would like to talk to Claude Pepper but he's embarrassingly New Frontier." Now, that stunned me because it was my first experience ever of someone saying, "He's embarrassingly on our side, so we don't want to talk to him." And it suddenly dawned on me that their feeling about the voter was like my feeling about beautiful scornful women. Any woman that liked me, something was wrong with her. And beautiful scornful women I wanted to seduce in the worst way. The Kennedy people constantly tried to win over people that didn't like them. And they had contempt for anybody who thought they were worth a shit. All you had to do was work hard for them to get on their shit list. So they seemed to me to be a joke, in the end.

There's an episode in that book where the judge provokes a public beating, and gets himself badly hurt, so he can turn it to political account when he finally gets out of the hospital. I have always wondered if there was any truth in that.

There is a basis of reality in that, though it did not involve a public beating. My father and his law partner got up at a big Fourth of July picnic where speeches were being made and said that the two of them would defend free of charge anybody who resisted the Klan in any way. Kill them, whatever. And they very shortly had cases and so on. They did, in fact, run the Klan out of Central Florida, and they were in great danger of being killed.

On the spot. The theatricality of that, putting your life on the line to make the play work properly, was something Ralegh might have done.

I think so. The Elizabethans have that sort of thing in common with the Southerners. It's a showboat way to take on the enemy, to really hit them right out there in the open. Something might have happened, but if it didn't happen right then, they were safe. As the only people who could possibly kill them were Klan people, and in those days, while you could die for doing shit like that, it sort of was a shield of protection to do it so publicly. By doing it quietly they might have easily have been burnt out or killed.

In the first couple of novels, did you feel like you needed to work for the market at all?

I didn't know what the market was. I had no idea what any of this was. I wanted *The Finished Man* to be kind of a straight novel. I wanted to learn how to do one. The way it got published at all in America was because the English had already accepted it. Scribners had rejected that novel. When they looked at the first hundred pages they said I didn't understand what a novel was like. I did nice short stories, but I had to understand that a novel had a beginning, a middle and an end to it, and my story as outlined didn't.

When Eyre and Spottiswoode took the book then Scribners wanted it also, and I added one thing to their manuscript that wasn't in Spottiswoode's. It took about five minutes. Three pages of manuscript—you'll see it in the book, if you open it up: Roman numeral I, BEGINNING (and a little epigraph); about midway through, II, MIDDLE; and in front of the last twenty pages, III, END. When they accepted it they said that I certainly had improved it a whole hell of a lot and had profited from their criticism. But rejection is my middle name—we could clutter up this whole interview with rejection stories.

Wasn't it in England that some publisher refused to believe you had written Which Ones Are the Enemy?

There was a furious letter, I wish I had it, saying that I was generous to a fault, but this was probably somebody else's novel, whom I was trying to help out. A cousin or something. They were outraged. But I wondered what they thought—if I were doing it for someone else, what was in it for all of us.

Anyway, some other English publisher did that one. The very first time I was ever in London, Susan and I got off the plane in the morning and the hotel room was not going to be ready until later in the afternoon; so we just kind of wandered around town. We didn't know where we were even. We were walking through an arcade and they had the first big bookshop that I saw in all of England. In the arcade and out in front they have several huge barrels. Unlike our little remainder things, they just dumped dead books in a barrel. A guy came out of the bookstore in like an undershirt wheeling a wheelbarrow full of *Which Ones Are the Enemy?* and dumped them in the barrel. You could get them for a dime apiece or something. Welcome to England, asshole!

Did you write that in the same way as The Finished Man?

Which Ones Are the Enemy? was an experiment in consistent voice. It is the only book I have ever written that was puffed up. Originally it was written on the advice of a friend with a possibility to get it published as a novella. We were back from Rome, in late 1959, and didn't have any money. I would do anything for a hundred dollars. The short novel possibility was five-hundred bucks or something—that was a lot of money. So I wrote it and then the series was canceled by whatever publisher was doing it and I was stuck with a sixty-page novella. Susan had had a new baby, and all the children got mumps or something, so she was sick and I stayed home for about a week, changing diapers on two babies, and in between I was sitting in the kitchen figuring out ways to take this novella and pump it into a novel.

How long did that take?

Time doesn't mean anything, but I couldn't possibly have worked on that book for more than about two weeks or so.

Did it make a difference to the tone of it, or to what happened?

I think a lot. Obviously, the more pressure there is on your time—you don't feel free enough to write something that would be so experimental that you doubt it could get published. It never occurred to me to try to make it difficult.

It's an alarmingly consistent voice. I've wondered how the idea came to you to write an entire novel in the voice of someone who seems such an evil bastard.

I never thought of this guy as an evil bastard. That's just a rhetorical device. I was fascinated by the habits of a first-person narrator who really has to make a case for himself because he's got a lot to be embarrassed about. You have to compare what he did and what happened with the way he told about it. And he, in fact, didn't do anything that bad at all, he just liked to describe it as a horrendously awful thing. This guy conceals his virtue behind a screen of vices. It was a variation on the unreliable narrator. You can't take his opinion as being wholly accurate.

That novel is set in Trieste but is contemporary with the Korean War. Doesn't the title come out of some Korean War episode?

That's a real story. These guys had all been in Korea, which was true of most of the people in Trieste. The reason I was in Trieste was they thought I had been in Korea, because of my serial number. All a complicated thing.

A guy in our outfit, who had been in Korea among the very first American troops, said that his outfit was up there fighting—dug in—and here came hundreds of Koreans, who waved and in effect communicated, "We are here to help." And it was really a great relief because they were hard pressed. They dug in all around him and then just before sunset they popped out of their foxholes and all began shooting the Americans. "Christ, it's the wrong ones. . . . "

His description of that thing and the whole beginning of the war was that way. A lot of guys lost a lot of their friends and a lot of pieces of themselves. But it was a funny story; they tried to make the best sport they could out of the fact.

I asked you about Southern writers influencing you, always a tiresome question, so now I will ask the same thing about war novelists.

At the time I was in the military, you couldn't get around the influence of James Jones, because everybody in the United States Army, starting in 1952, read *From Here to Eternity*. It didn't change either their attitude or what they did, but they did it referentially, in terms of *From Here to Eternity*. They would say, "Boy, you are going to get the

From Here to Eternity treatment. We are going to kick your ass just like they did Prewitt." So it became a literary allusion even as they did it.

You've written a lot about war, both in Which Ones Are the Enemy? *and in the historical novels. Do you have any general notions about it at all?*

I have never been in a real war. The only thing that I can claim that I share with people who have been in sustained combat is having been shot at. I know what that's like. You do get the idea that they're trying to kill you.

My own feeling is, first thing, that it is enormously appealing. Even if you have had some experience of it. I suspect that if I had been in the First World War and done a year or two in the trenches I would feel differently. Otherwise, I think the greatest thing said about it was Robert E. Lee's remark: "It is well that war is so terrible, else we should love it too much." People love the excitement of being at risk and the pleasure of killing other people.

Why do you think that is?

I don't know—it comes with the animal, I think.

Walker Percy might call it the reptile brain at work.

Maybe so. It's like denying original sin to deny that that pleasure and that excitement are clearly in the world. There must be fifty separate wars going on right this minute while we're talking.

The problem with it is not, "How do you feel about killing somebody?" The real problem is, "How do you feel about being killed?" Most people that I have run into would do anything, including boil their mothers in oil, to avoid being killed. This is a basic twentieth-century truth—we have learned it again and again.

It seems to me that in your third novel, Do, Lord, Remember Me, *the oral quality becomes much stronger; the voice begins to take over and is impossible to ignore. And the multiple viewpoints come into it. In structure, it looks forward more than the others do. Any reason for that?*

Well, you're right about that, I guess. One difference from the earlier books was that some of the pressures on me to write more conventionally did not exist. With *Do, Lord, Remember Me* I had no desire to make it simple. I had a job. So therefore I was liberated to try stuff I wanted to do. The version that was printed represented half of that book. Fifty percent of it was cut out. I was under contract to Little, Brown, and I sent in this novel and didn't hear from them for a long time. And back it came two days before Christmas, 1963, with a very short letter that said, "Goodbye, we don't need this. We find this novel to be scabrous and orotund." I will never forget the term, "scabrous and orotund." I had to get a dictionary to find out if that was good or not. That was Alan D. Williams, and at some point he said, "Don't give up. Some day you will make a dent in the American consciousness." Ever since then I have seen it as a fender, this huge fender— the American consciousness.

Doubleday then took *Do, Lord* on a one-shot basis. They wanted it shorter and I cut it. It was one of those stories with two separate plots that come together and the easiest way to cut was to take one of them out. The one I took out was comic, much more comic than the book that exists now. The long version would have been better.

Death of the Fox and The Succession *were also cut in half, weren't they?*

More or less, yes.

By you or by the publisher?

By me. They had suggestions, some of which I took, some of which I didn't. They didn't demand anything except that it should come in at a certain page count.

Would the long versions of those books have been better?

I don't know. Maybe they would not have held up at the length they were written. There was a lot that was eminently terrible.

It looks like, especially once you started working on the long novels, that you must have been working on a lot of different things at once. Does it happen, when a novel won't work or becomes frustrating, that you switch off and work on stories or poems?

Oh, yeah. That's also a sort of safety valve, working on several things. There are a lot of things that don't work for me. But the older I get, the less I want to allow them not to work. I want to find a way. Way back, if something didn't work right away, I just threw it out as if it was a dumb idea, and went on to something else. So I was very spendthrift at that time, but those things resurface anyway. You forget all about them, but they come back in another form. But that's true—if you're working on enough different things there is always something you can do. It allows you to escape the total blank page, and total silence, though both of those may be very attractive.

Are there any procedural differences in the way you work on different kinds of things: stories, poems, long ten-year novels, shorter two-or-three-year novels?

The only thing I can say is that nothing has been very much alike. Even the historical novels are significantly different, I think. Therefore, all I learn from doing a book when I finish it is how I should have done it in the first place. It doesn't carry over to the next book. The next book is different. So, I'm always looking for new procedures. Each time it's a new situation. The things that are carried over are slighter and of less significance than the new problems, the things that I have never encountered before.

I suspect some of this is the result of teaching writing a long time, that it is a way of getting over self-consciousness. If I were doing the same thing all the time, I might be more self-conscious or habitual about it. It's almost as if an inner voice sent me to try to do different things each time so I wouldn't be able to fall back on habit, so I wouldn't get bored and communicate excessive boredom the way a coach or teacher might, going through the same motions all of the time.

What is the first thing you began to write, poetry or fiction?

Poems. Back in the early forties, high school and college. I got a lot of readings when I was still in college, which was kind of a new thing. But it didn't even occur to me to try to publish that stuff. My first exposure was reading out loud to an audience, and I did that for quite a little while before getting anything published. That was always the primary basis of everything—the oral. And that makes for a different kind of poem, in a way.

Early on, in some kind of collegiate contest, Marianne Moore was one of the judges, and she got to be a friend. That was in her reclusive stage. She was asked to introduce a younger poet at the Museum of Modern Art, and since she didn't know anybody else, she introduced me. In those days, I thought that was perfectly natural: of course I would be taken to the Museum of Modern Art and introduced by Marianne Moore. I went on the fumes of that a long time. It was much later, four or five years, that I ever thought about publishing anything.

So you were just reading, not even sending a poem out to a magazine?

I published some in the *Nassau Lit*, which was really important to me. I knew so little that when those things appeared I would swagger around thinking I was world famous.

I didn't worry so much about how things looked on the page because I was working with sound. The poems were out of sync with what everybody else was doing at that time because they were mostly writing a formal verse. They were writing stuff to be read on the page and a characteristic of the poetry of that kind, with Lowell and a lot of the rest of them, was the difficulty of discerning what the poem was supposed to be about. What was the action of poem, what was the situation. Part of the game of that poetry was the discovery: "Oh, this is a poem about tennis!" That didn't interest me at all. When you are reading out loud to an audience, and they are not reading the text and pondering over it, the one thing they have got to know is the situation and the event. If you are getting a response directly on the spot from an audience, then you are perfectly willing to throw away the front of the poem in order to get where you are going to go. In effect, the unit becomes the whole poem, rather than the flashy lines. It also moves more toward punch-line; it's built a little like a joke. It builds as a narrative can build. Lyric exalted feeling has nowhere special to go.

Charles Israel says that he draws parallels between your poetry and the work of Ralegh and the Elizabethan poets. Is there any merit in that suggestion?

I would be delighted if there was. I certainly did read a lot of it. I had my little book of the metaphysical poets—I carried it around the way George Barker carries *A Shropshire Lad.* Then it was a relief to come to Ralegh—he had a lot of the same moves that Donne did, but you didn't have to be a master of the old science to understand it, there weren't all those highly intellectual allusions. Lately it has been as a result of writing about the Elizabethan period that I have come to like the sixteenth-century poets more, and understand them.

One of the things I liked about the metaphysicals and particularly about Ralegh was the rapid shifts of tone. Fast cutting, you might call it, where you're in one rhetoric one second and another one the next. The best example of that being the last lines of "Passionate Man's Pilgrimage," which I keep coming back to.

Can you quote that?

I can give you some of it:

> And this is my eternal plea,
> To him that made Heaven, Earth, and Sea,
> Seeing my flesh must die so soon,
> And want a head to dine next noon,
> Just at the stroke when my veins start and spread
> Set on my soul an everlasting head.

And then a throwaway ending:

> Then I am ready like a palmer fit,
> To tread those blest paths which before I writ.

The most vivid physical description of a beheading I know of, very realistic, with that bravado—those fast moves. If you make fast moves in tone, quick cuts, you are also using a variety of languages. Right within those eight lines there are several levels, moving from the colloquial to the rhetorical to the grandiose and back down. That interested me a whole lot.

Okay, the standard thing being done when I started, and there are still people around doing it, was done most effectively by, say, Richard Wilbur. He was a poet I admired enormously but didn't see anything much in common with. His method was mostly development of one tone, one voice. His only gags or games were more intellectual. He loved puns, sort of functional puns that you hear a lot at the ends of his poems as he wrapped them up. They were quite beautiful, which you can't be in the way that I'm talking about. You can have a beautiful line. But you can't have a beautiful poem if you are going to jump around in language.

The prevailing mode of the time was the poem as finished object, more like a piece of sculpture—you walk around it. The poems that I was trying to write were meant to give the impression (it's equally artificial) of spontaneously happening now. The poem is making itself up even as you are doing it. The two presuppositions are utterly different in what you are aiming for. And you can miss very badly with the wrong cut or shift of tone; you can blow the whole poem.

The characteristic poetry of the period was poetry built around the line as unit. And in the poem I'm talking about, the poem that's working itself out, to have a finished line would go completely against the grain of what you are pretending is happening. So nothing falls into place until you get to the end. The lines tend to tumble and tend to be unfinished.

Is it reasonable to say that the formal poems you wrote earlier and the seemingly looser ones that come later are both constructed—

—on the same theory. The same theoretical thing is behind them, whether they are formal or loose.

Was there any reason for your shifting from a high style to a comparatively colloquial voice in the verse?

Looking back now, the clearest line that I can see has to do with the relationship of the prose and the poetry. That is, when I was writing short stories or quasi-realistic novels about the Army and politics and stuff, I was writing rather formal, old-fashioned sorts of verse. When I started working on these long novels, working with a language that, while I hope it isn't stilted, is certainly removed from colloquial day-to-day English, the verse got loose. To satisfy my own need to be in touch with my own language at the time that I am living, I wrote more and more of what you might call casual and colloquial verse. It also happened to be, unfortunately, opposite from what everyone else was doing at any given time. I have never been in sync (I would gladly be in sync if I could) with whatever movements were going on.

What do you think of these movements and things?

What's bad about it is that each group pretends that none of the others exist. The careerists at the moment seem to have closed their minds to everything except what they are doing—moneychangers in the temple.

Why is that?

Well, there's one practical fact: it is worthwhile now for the first time in the twentieth century to be a careerist in poetry, because there are a few rewards, for the few, that are significant. Teaching jobs and grants and prizes and so forth. Until this present generation of poets, poetry had not been anything but a means toward downward mobility. There wasn't anything in it for anybody.

Okay, there are rewards, but not much; there aren't enough jobs or grants to take care of all the poets. So there is a temptation to belong to a group that has some power and prestige and is able to reward you. And there is a temptation to close one's eyes to anything outside of that. I do know, for example, that it makes my friend and esteemed colleague Charles Wright extremely nervous to either hear about or talk about poets he doesn't know. He doesn't want to hear that there are unknown poets in Texas right now. I remember Jim Dickey categorically asserting that there couldn't be life in outer space, but what he had in mind was that he didn't want there to be any poets out there. Right now, writing stuff he didn't know about. It's sort of like a small trough with a lot of pigs trying to get up there, and it makes these people nervous, it takes their concentration away, to have in the back of their minds that right this minute, at desks all over America, poets they never heard of are writing in styles they don't know how to use. That's enough to really throw the old writer's block on a lot of people.

Now the next aspect of this, which is much more serious than pure careerism, is that it is either you make it or it's back to the old cotton field or assembly line for a lot of these guys. So I have known a lot of young poets coming out of Iowa or somewhere who very patiently wait their turn because if they don't they're going to be out in left field, somewhere that no one is looking at them. You get in a hierarchical club like the Iowa or Breadloaf circuit, and even if you are not one of their stars, if you stay patient and do what we used to call "pulling wool" down South, your time will come. They can't leave you unrewarded forever. Queen Elizabeth could, but the Iowa Writers Workshop can't.

You've done a lot of editing over the years, the Transatlantic Review, *the* Contemporary Poetry Series *for North Carolina, and so forth. Did you ever feel like you were looking for anything in particular, certain styles, or whatever?*

No. Ideally, I would want to claim I was an open and eclectic editor. But that claim tells you that I wanted to appear to myself that way, so therefore I would probably not have been as receptive as I might to a good piece of fashionable work.

You've taught at a lot of different schools and there must be hundreds of publishing writers who've had you as a teacher at one time or another. Do you think writing can be taught?

Well, you can't teach anybody to be a writer. I never had somebody say, "Make me a writer!" I have had close to it, one guy who said, "I will do anything to be one." All you had to do was tell him to do something once and he would do it, and this was a horrendous responsibility, because he didn't resist. Other than that I have mostly had people who needed response, needed direction or something to come up against, but who were not to be made into writers. You can teach certain kinds of techniques, the way that people teach the violin and the cello.

My approach to this is rather like that of my late uncle Jack, the golf pro, who was supposed to be one of the great golf teachers. He was one of the first guys in the history of golf to get holistic about it. He didn't know the word, but he suddenly realized that all this discussion— "this is the grip, and this is the stance"—was working against the experience of hitting the golf ball. So instead he took people out with a bucket of balls and just had them start hitting that ball. He wouldn't give them much advice at all because what he was trying to find out was what their natural body inclinations were. Basically, all you are then is a critic, you are not imposing a system.

I picked up a class right after a very arbitrary, directive teacher had left, who had told them, "The following things are in a short story and should be in your short story. And I will not read stories on the following subjects . . . " We worked as kind of a nice one-two team: when I came in I said, "Anything is a short story, let's see what you got." And then worked in terms of what they did. And that is my whole method, such as it is. So you don't end up saying that you taught anybody. You responded to somebody—they taught themselves. And for writers, maybe that's the best way.

In a sense that was my editorial method. I always felt that the writer knew the work best. And so I never had any suggestions on how to fix it unless they asked me. A lot of editors work another way: they volunteer that your work needs fixing and they are going to do it.

When we first started the *Transatlantic Review* we solicited work, not in the way it's usually solicited: "We'd love to see some poems by you with the hope of publishing them." My pitch was, "We are going to publish anything you send us." Out of that I got off-beat stuff, some very good things that the writers liked, but their fans and other editors maybe didn't, stuff they felt pretty strongly about. Only one or two writers in that whole period of the magazine sent me a bummer. Real bad. Junk. And we published it.

To their everlasting shame.

Alas, there is no such thing. Shame lasts about five minutes in the literary world.

Do you have any favorite thing out of all the work you've done?

No. I always pretend to prefer the latest.

Looking over the record, your career has seemed to run in cycles of publication and recognition. Several books a year at the beginning, and you won the Prix de Rome. Then nearly a decade without much happening. Then Death of the Fox makes the best-seller list. Another decade of virtual silence, and now you've got four or five new books out, with The Succession, *maybe, in the lead. The wheel of fortune has made a couple of complete revolutions in your case, it would seem. What do you think of the literary life?*

It's a mug's game, as Eliot called it. That part, that's not very satisfactory. Why I thought it would be immune from the general scriptural description of life on this earth I don't know. I imagined that by writing I would somehow be immune from the normal course of things, which leads inevitably to contempt for the mundane. So the literary life is, of course, rich with disappointments. It's disappointing that I allow myself to be disappointed.

It's taken me a long time to figure this out, and other people have known it all along in a slightly different way, but it's what my wife, Susan, says: "Public life does not exist. Only private life is real. Public life of any kind is an illusion." I'm not sure that's true. . . .

Ralegh might not have agreed with that.

No, I think not either. Except, when he came out of the courtroom the day before he died, having been sentenced to death again in Westminster, a cousin of his saw that he was being very witty with a lot of the people, with jokes and bursts of laughter. The cousin said it was very unseemly for a guy just condemned to death to be cracking jokes, and Ralegh, punning at the time, said, "Indulge me a little, I shall be grave enough at the sad parting."

Lack of recognition does affect what you do. And you find yourself desiring trashy things. The hideous irony is that you box yourself in a position where if you get what you've been waiting for, it turns out to be a nice platter of trash.

Faulkner has been a great inspiration to me, an influence in the sense that he managed to succeed in doing his work while being bitterly unhappy—and it's quite clear that he was—over not getting any kind of recognition. My favorite example is from the unpublished introduction to *The Sound and the Fury*. He had enormous difficulty with his third novel, which ultimately became *Sartoris*, in terms of getting it published anywhere. So he had this tremendous disappointment, because things had been real easy up to that point. And he says he was liberated to write *The Sound and the Fury* by having this thing happen to him. He said, "One day I seemed to close a door on all agents, publishers, book lists, and everything else, and said to myself—now I can write." It's the reverse of doors being closed in your face. You close the door.

Did you ever wish you had not done this, and instead had made your career as a Marine fighter pilot or something of the sort?

I really liked certain aspects of the Army life, and I thought for a while that I might just do that. I was a master sergeant at the end of it. I looked around and there were some master sergeants that had a pleasant life. But I'd probably be very dead by this time. I didn't know the Vietnam War was coming.

With all the irritations and frustrations that come with being a full-time professional writer, do you still think it's worth it?

Nobody chooses. There's a poem by David Slavitt, "The Calf and the Ox," based on a fable of Avianus, where a frisky little calf is standing by the fence and laughing at this big dumb ox, yoked and pulling a heavy plow. In his cheerful amusement the calf doesn't see "the farmer who carries a glittering butcher knife / and a light halter, coming toward the calf." And then the last line of the poem, the old-fashioned moral, is, "Nobody gets to choose which yoke to wear." And I know that's true.

Your major choices, such as they are, are always made without any real knowledge of where they may lead, and you tell yourself that, as in "The Road Not Taken." You're going to say, as Frost does in the poem, "I took the one less traveled by, / And that has made all the difference," But he makes it quite clear that he didn't know whether it was less traveled or not, so he was not capable of making that conclusion. What I would choose, knowing what I know now, would still be chosen in ignorance and would probably turn out to be equally disappointing. So it seems to me a great relief that nobody gets to choose which yoke to wear.

A Letter to the Students
of the University of Virginia

One of these days, sooner rather than later, you are going to walk into an entrance of Cabell Hall and notice the inscription over it. It says: "Here we are not afraid to follow Truth wherever it may lead nor to tolerate any error so long as reason is left free to combat it." That is a stunning, startling, shining statement of this university's pure and simple purpose as envisioned by its honored founder. Those words are like a musical accompaniment for your mind to dance to. They are intended to set your spirit free and soaring like the statue of that naked guy with the funny hat and the cockamamie wings (James R. McConnell, '10) by the library. Take a good look at him and the inscription over that Cabell doorway and then try your best to remember them and how you felt the first time you encountered them.

You are going to find that a large majority of the faculty, grumpy and cynical anyway, what with their salary cuts and all, have only a dim memory of those words. *If* they ever noticed them. You are also going to find out that the (pardon the expression) administrators, you know, deans and people like that, are so busy with their numbers games and their shuffling paperwork and their hard labor—administration is puzzling work for people who have never, until now, managed anything as large and complex as an infantry rifle squad—that they don't know what is over *any* of the doors around here; as long as it isn't a string of spray-painted obscenities, they couldn't care less. (By the way, speaking of salaries. Under the law, and I mean the Law, it is your right to know the salaries of any and all faculty and administrators. Why not exercise that right from time to time?)

Many Politically Correct People, hereinafter to be called PCP, including a significant percentage of the faculty and even a few terrified and hypnotized students, know about the words, more or less. Trouble is, the PCP strongly oppose them. They say that "reason" is just a buzzword made up by generations of brutal White Male Oppressors (WMO) to take advantage of and to exploit everybody else. These WMO invented all kinds of bogus stuff, see?, like logic and syntax and grammar and arithmetic and all that kind of crapola to keep the rest of society and the whole wide world with all its fun-loving, life-affirming, intuitive, shucking-and-jiving population in a state of perpetual confusion and involuntary servitude. And as for that great-big-old-humongous capitalized word, "Truth," PCP tend to agree with that bona fide celebrity (after all, his name is prayerfully repeated by millions of people every day and even more so on Sunday) Pontius Pilate. He knew that questions are more important than answers. Look him up sometime if you can find a Bible around here.

Okay. So some students, a lot of the faculty, and most of the (pardon) administration, without even looking up and considering those words (and not counting a significant percentage of our semiprofessional jocks, for whom the sentence is much too long and complicated, anyway), go on about their daily chores and mischief as if the Founder had never lived and come up with that one and a lot of other cute and irrelevant sayings way back then when, BC as we say, looking sadly at boarded up frat houses, meaning Before Cocaine.

No wonder that winged nudist can't get it off the ground.

Welcome to UVA, kiddos, and to charming old Charlottesville.

Hold tight to your wallet the whole time you're here. And try to sit everywhere (except maybe the Eastern Standard and the C & O) with your back to the wall.

Who is this guy? you are wondering. You have a perfect right to ask if you have read this far. Good question. My name is John Towne. And I am not a student or a member of the faculty or even (praise the Lord and pardon the expression) an administrator. I am just a character. I mean exactly that. I am a real character who lives mostly in a novel (*Poison Pen*, 1986) and several nondescript short stories. My author (read: Slavemaster) was supposed to write this piece to welcome you to UVA and C'ville. But he was too chicken and he couldn't hack it. Like a whole lot of his so-called colleagues (you'll find out—oh, boy), he is, at the present time, disgruntled, disillusioned, and more or less dysfunctional. He is also, in the words of one of his colleagues in the English Department (a true child of the Thrilling 1960s), "completely irrelevant." Let me assure you that you wouldn't want to listen to him even if he were (that's an example of the subjunctive; look it up) able to write a couple of rational sentences without blowing his cover or his cool. Like old Pilate, he has washed his hands of this little task. So I took over. It's better this way. You can trust me. I've got nothing to lose. My author is afraid he'll lose his parking sticker in B-1 and maybe his office with the window in it if he levels with you. My author is an old guy and getting older every day. But being a fictional character, I can stay the same way always. I keep the same consistent character, also. I will never change much. Some critics and reviewers think that's not such a good thing. They think I am not a good role model or even a very nice person.

Would you like to know some of the things they have called me, those crummy (pardon the expression) critics? Sure you would. Glad you asked. *The New York Times Book Review* referred to me as "a low life crank." *The Chicago Tribune* described me as "a lecherous, misanthropic, failed academic." *The Village Voice* identified me as "an exceptionally sleazy picaro." Do you know what the good old, down-home *Greensboro News* said about me? They said I was "a loathsome, racist, sexist, crude and gruesome creep." Enough of that kind of thing could hurt a guy's feelings, even a sensitive guy like me.

That reminds me. If you want to make out like a bandit while you are here, cultivate your sensitivity, raise your drooping consciousness, be open and vulnerable, protest poverty, mortality, and injustice everywhere except in Albemarle County (there is Third-World-style poverty within fifteen minutes of the dome of the Rotunda in any and all directions, but please don't talk about that), and don't write too many bum checks. They tend to take commerce seriously around here.

If you begin to be more or less successful in your program of making out, regardless of any particular sexual preference, you will soon discover there are caches of condoms everywhere. But more important than that by far is full mutual agreement and understanding between you and your partner. Maybe a simple contract will cover it. Or maybe a covert tape recording. True, these little details tend to reduce the level of romantic excitation (love?), but better safe than sorry and sitting in the slammer. Know what I mean?

That brings up the whole matter of the Honor System. They are somewhat serious about that. Unless you are a big-time jock or something, it is, on the whole, probably better not to lie, steal, and cheat while you are here at UVA. Don't get caught at it, anyway. And if you do get yourself caught, do not pass Go, go directly to the Law School where you can easily, cheaply, find counsel ready, willing, and able to tie up your case in the sweet flypaper of procedural errors. Or, if you are a little lucky, you can obtain the services of a PCP who will attack the whole system, arguing that the word "honor" was invented by WMOs to deprive others of their traditional fun and games, petty and grand larceny. Worst case scenario? Cry a lot. That proves sensitivity. At the same time, between deep and heartfelt sobs, feel free to point out the obvious—that the Honor System does not apply to faculty or (*pardonnez-moi*) administrators or anybody else except unwitting students. So much for the Honor System. Think of it as an anachronism.

Maybe another word or two about the PCP at UVA is in order. Frankly, it's a problem for everyone. I mean, you know and I know how it can easily mean the difference between a B and an A as your grade in any given course. Of course, it doesn't really apply (not yet anyway—there are busy folks working to change that) to hard and practical subjects like math, the sciences, and engineering. Those people deal in numbers and stuff like that. But unless you are totally and irrevocably committed to Navajo Math or Yoruba Geometry, you'll probably do all right in science and engineering courses around here.

It is in the precincts of the so-called Liberal Arts that the PCP have hunkered down like Saddam Hussein in his bunker. It's hard to believe, but they are really and truly dead serious about all this PC stuff. The way people used to be about the Honor System and religion and the dress code and other legendary concerns.

(Dress Code . . . Please excuse the digressive interruption, but digression is the essence of my style. There is no real, official dress code around here. Nevertheless on any given day everybody dresses almost exactly alike, about as alike as the Keydets over at VMI. Except, of course, for the usual nerds and wimps. All real people seem to get the message as to what is the appropriate uniform of the day, and they wear it, too. I do not know, yet, how that message is sent out to the entire university. If anyone already knows or finds out, please phone me, John Towne, at 924-6675.)

Okay. Back to PCP. You probably thought all that stuff mattered only at tony, trendy places like Duke (the Albania of academe) or the Ivy League, places you always wanted to get in and go to but couldn't. Hey, don't feel bad. You could have ended up some place like Vanderbilt. But UVA is just as PC, at least in the Liberal Arts, as any of those places. We are just more polite about it. We place a premium on good manners. Be Politically Correct, but be sure to pepper your dialogue with "Sir" and "Ma'am." And remember to stand up when a grownup Feminoid enters the room. Use a knife and fork if they give you one or the other. Don't break wind in class, at least while the teacher is talking. On the other hand, it can be a good tactic when some nerdy, bow-head student is trying to make points with the teacher.

You may think you aren't really ready to be PC yet. Don't worry or fret. It's easy. You could understand *Thelma and Louise*, couldn't you? Sure, there are a couple of funny lines in there you are not really supposed to laugh at, but you can learn. If you ever do laugh at anything PC or at any PCP, try and do so in the dark. Then if they catch you, follow the time-honored practice of the Congress of the United States—deny everything and allege fraud.

Actually, the essentials of PC are easy. There are only a few basic things you need to know. Women and minorities are good. White men are bad, at least until they get themselves trained in sensitivity and self-abnegation. Everything good and worthwhile about modern political life—the Constitution, the Bill of Rights, the Warren Court, as well as more complex stuff like Physics, Chemistry, Astronomy, Philosophy, etc.—all originated deep in the heart of the Third World. But the thing is they were so busy and happy singing and dancing that they forgot all that, while the lazy Europeans, living in their cold caves, with nothing else to do but sit around and brood and think, ripped it off and since then have used it to make life miserable for everybody else, including you, too, UVA students, having to go away from home to college and study a lot of different things (as well as party a lot) before you can finally get your degree and get a high-paying and easy job somewhere.

Got it? PC is easy, see?

If you want to go for it and earn an A+, in whatever course, you may have to take a little risk. Pretend at first that you disagree with your teacher. Not very much and not for long. Disagree, briefly and slightly; then, blaming everything on your parents, become a convert to PC. We call it the Lost Sheep Ploy, after something or other about sheep in the Bible.

I know, I know, there are too many sheep in the Bible. Those old guys had a thing about sheep. Sheep couldn't talk back to them or tell on them. Say, have you seen that bumper sticker—"Hampden-Sydney / Where The Men Are Men / And The Sheep Are Scared"?

And if you ever get in trouble with PCP, always bear in mind that we have something called The First Amendment Institute (or something like that). Some smartmouths have nicknamed it (for obscure reasons) the White Elephants' Graveyard. But the whole thing is that they are actually there and are publicly in favor of the

First Amendment (more or less and except for stuff like this article). They might even help you if you got into trouble for something you write in a paper or say out loud in class. Don't count on it, though. They will always defend to the death (yours) the right to say the F-word anywhere you want to and can get away with it. But everything beyond that is (pardon) ambiguous. The better part of wisdom is to Watch What You Think. Don't ever think anything that isn't PC, and then you won't end up saying things that will get you low grades and the haughty and imperious disdain of the PCP.

Hey, but I have been giving you the wrong impression by talking about academic things so much. Traditionally academic life is only a small part of the UVA experience. As you knew before you even applied, social activity is much more important and time consuming. Now, it may be a little bit intimidating at first when you are new here, witnessing all those suave, young, attractive people in their stylish clothes, watching them drive around in their very expensive cars. You'll see they know how to find parking places and order wine in a restaurant and things like that. They seem to know exactly what to wear when they go jogging and jiggling up and down Rugby Road. But don't let them fool you. You do not have to be intimidated. Very, very few of your classmates and almost none of the faculty and administration will ever be found in that ultimate arbiter of arrival—*The Social Register*. The overwhelming majority, here at UVA, are dedicated social wannabees. And if they work hard at it and behave themselves, maybe their grandchildren will make it inside that social winners circle.

But is it worth it? I mean, look at it this way. How socially intimidating can any place be that has a former belly dancer and a guy who used to run a chain of nude dancing establishments on its Board of Visitors? They set the tone and example. So, relax. As long as you don't get arrested for child abuse or serious dope dealing you can hold up your head with pride at UVA.

I know I can. And I am only a character who has briefly escaped from between the covers of an obscure book.

To which I must (alas) now return.

Listen.

Before I go.

UVA is beautiful—more so than most places. Enjoy it.

The Founder was a great human being. His works and words are worth remembering and thinking about once in a while. You could do worse.

And that naked man with the wings on his arms down there in front of Clemons Library. People still touch parts of him for luck on exams. But he is something more than that. He is the dream, the spirit of the dreamer. It takes courage to dream true dreams. It took courage and *chutzpah* to get naked and to strap on those huge wings. You want a role model? Well, there he is. One of these days he will flap his wings and fly away. You will want to be there and see it and applaud.

Meantime, if anybody wants to applaud me ("Towne tells it like it is!"), call 924-6675 and leave a message for me.

Have a good day.

As for me? Thank you, but I have other plans.

When Lorena Bobbitt Comes Bob-Bob-Bobbing Along: The Sorry State of Popular Culture

Dear Howard Stern,

I don't care if your New Year's Eve program did set the all-time world's record for a pay-for-view TV event. And I don't care, either, if your book is a bestseller and people are lining up around the block to get a signed copy of it. I just want to tell you, in all candor, than you are an ugly person. Ugly, *Ugly*, UGLY. You are as *ugly* as a raw turnip. Ugly as a day-old dog turd. Next to you that fat slob Rush Limbaugh looks like Clark Gable. You are ugly inside and outside both. Quit hiding behind ethnicity. That's no excuse. Your hippie hairdo doesn't do a thing for you, either. Why don't you get smart and go find a good place to hide instead of flaunting your ugliness in the florid face of the American public?

As a member in good standing of the South Carolina Ugly Patrol (an all-volunteer, nonprofit statewide organization dedicated to the proposition that "Beauty is Truth") I am compelled in good conscience to write to you. . . .

Stop, please. Wait just a minute!

Please forgive me, dear reader. It was not I who wrote
the above rude and counterproductive words addressed
to one of America's cultural icons and leading celebrities.
I, myself, would never do such a thing. True, I might
conceivably *think* something like that, but would never
allow myself to give voice and utterance to such negative
thoughts. In my opinion it was Towne, John Towne, no
more (and no less) than a common character in a novel I
once wrote called *Poison Pen* (1986), a fictional figure,
then, who has just lately reemerged, all bandaged and
stinking, like Lazarus, from the quiet death of that novel
to begin again his outrageous and unacceptable shenani-
gans, his half-assed japes and pasquils, his minstrel show
shucking and jiving, always and forever seeking to give
offense not only to the vulnerable and prominent people
he has elected to insult, but also, dear readers (if any), to
you and to me and to every right-thinking human being
from here to Sri Lanka. You may be thinking that I, as a
bona fide author of sorts (though never either celebrity or
bestseller), ought at the very least to be able to exercise
some kind of control over a purely imaginary character
whose sole existence (as far as I can tell) is in words on
the printed page, whose environment is his text. Maybe
so. It just hasn't worked out that way, that's all. He
comes and he goes as he pleases. He pops up when least
expected. Like some of my tacky, no-account kinfolk.
Since he appears to have vanished (for the time being) let
us now get down to serious business, to the topic of
Popular Culture, while we can still safely do so.

What a time to be thinking about this subject; what a
time to be trying to write about it. My imaginary readers
will be reading this piece a couple or three months from
now, on the early teasing edges of springtime. But I am
living here and now, composing this text in early January
of 1994. It is a frozen, grungy day outside, gray on gray,

with clumps of old snow in all directions, and if the weather report is to be believed, more snow on the way. Nothing much going on out there in the neighborhood. Not a dog barking, not a car growling up the hill outside. Not even the demented woodwind noise of the usual black caucus of crows anywhere nearby. Inside, I have the newspapers with their annual lists of what's "In" and what's "Out." I gather from the *Washington Post*'s half-serious consideration of the topic that Heidi Fleiss, Janet Malcolm, Donald and Marla, Robert Reich, and many more are In. Evidently the Out basket contains the likes of Joey and Amy, Richard Gere, Catherine MacKinnon, and to be sure, Clarence Thomas. However, the big news is found a few pages later under the rubric of "Names & Faces." "Michael Does Vegas" says the headline. The brief story tells how Michael Jackson, identified as "beleaguered pop star," appeared in person to watch "a Las Vegas casino pirate show" in the company of the casino owner, somebody named Steve Wynn, together with (are you ready for this?) "junk bond king Michael Milken, along with a phalanx of security guards." "Phalanx," that's a nice touch. In the morning's mail came *Vanity Fair* with its lead article—"Heidi Does Hollywood." Which I don't have to read, anyway, because the Associated Press has a piece in the papers—"*Vanity Fair* names names in Fleiss story"—where I can quickly learn that customer Charlie Sheen "liked to hire a blonde dressed up in a cheerleader outfit who would pretend she had a big game the next day, Fleiss said." My *New York Times* tells me all about a popular new video game, *Police Quest: Open Season*, designed and created by Daryl Gates, late of the Los Angeles Police Department.

In short, friends, the world looks to be cuckoo. Bananas. . . .

Interruptions flutter a few similar days (like those blowing calendar pages in old timey movies), grungy, still gray on gray, and I can read in *The Washington Post*, in the front *news* section, mind you, how "ROCK MUSICIAN'S CONVICTION PROMPTS CANCELLATION OF AD ON CONDOM USE." This is a little glitch in the major radio and TV advertising campaign, sponsored by the Centers for Disease Control and Prevention, part of the Department of Health and Human Services, which, in its lofty wisdom, "has ordered the immediate withdrawal of its AIDS-prevention public service announcement for radio featuring Red Hot Chili Peppers singer Anthony Kiedis." Seems that this fellow, this spokesperson for clean living and good behavior, had earlier been convicted (in a real live courtroom—Fairfax County Circuit Court) of "sexual battery and indecent exposure." Since it is her bailiwick and the buck always stops somewhere, Dona Shalala had to come up with something: "We must not allow a single ad to overshadow the vital lifesaving message in the campaign."

Dear Miz Shalala,

When the poet Marianne Moore, in her poem "In Distrust of Merits," said "Beauty is everlasting and dust is for a time," she said a mouthful. . . .

—Go away, Towne! My readers don't want to listen to you anymore. Be reasonable.
—Okay, boss. I was just leaving, anyway. May I make one point, though, what I was fixing to say in my letter to Madame Secretary?
—Go ahead but make it quick.
—Have you ever noticed that our American presidents, at least the ones of our lifetime, like to surround

themselves with people of certain definite types? Roosevelt liked smartmouth intellectuals; Truman liked laughers and scratchers; Kennedy liked Harvard men and lace-curtain Irish; Johnson liked little bitty short guys like Jack Valenti and Moyers, it made him feel taller than ever; Carter liked undisguised crackers, etc., etc. What's the Clinton pattern?

—Beats me.

—Ugly. He has surrounded himself with some of the most singularly unattractive people ever collected. It makes him feel better about himself, don't you see? Bye-bye. . . .

Where were we?

Oh, yes, stories in the papers. Well, the big news today, prominently on page one as well as the "Style" section of *The Washington Post*, is the Lorena Bobbitt trial, just getting underway at historic Manassas. (The San Antonio trial of some of the leftover Branch Davidians gets a lot less attention. No celebrities involved.) The Bobbitt event is described as big-time show business: "About 20 satellite trucks lined the roadway leading to the courthouse yesterday, and vendors turned the walk-way into a carnival midway, hawking commemorative T-shirts, boxer shorts, knives and penis-shaped choco-lates."

"What does all this have to do with Popular Culture in the dear old U.S. of A.?" you ask.

Reader, *this* is *Popular Culture*. This is what it has come to. And if I get half a chance between interruptions, I am going to try to tell you how and why it has come to pass.

Dear Mrs. Bobbitt,

Looking at your picture in the paper today, my good
friend Richard allowed: "Boy, that looks like a woman
that would cut your dick off." He's right, too, but please
don't get us wrong. We have just founded a local chapter
of the Lorena Bobbitt Marching Society and Fan Club. I
thought you would like to know that there are guys who
admire and respect you as well as the feminist gals.
Today's *Washington Post*, in the "Style" section says (in a
subheadline) "As Lorena's Trial Begins, Women Grab
Onto a Powerful New Symbol." So? Guys, too. We are
grabbing and holding onto our symbols, too, for dear
life. . . .

Something happened in the four generations of this
century to change forever a popular culture that was
essentially local, spontaneous, essentially amateur when
compared and contrasted with the present, though modest amounts of money did indeed change hands from time
to time. At the beginning of the century only opera
singers and stage actors were "stars" in a contemporary
sense. Both of those forms, opera and drama, were parts
of the national and international popular culture of the
time. Both are now merely shadows of themselves. Both
are classified as "elitist" entertainment, together with
symphony orchestras and art museums, subsidized and
supported by taxes and philanthropy. Where in the late
nineteenth century most forms of culture of any kind
were local and regional, there was scarcely an American
town that did not at least have a theater and an opera
house. Now only the largest of cities, and only some of
them, still try to continue to enjoy these once-popular
arts.

What followed, at first gradually enough, was the development of technology (movies, radio, television, cable television, videos, computer networks), which by linking us all together, like it or not, destroyed most of the earlier kinds of popular culture we had known, replacing these things with professionally controlled production and distribution of products that had only a shadowy relationship with original, authentic popular and folk culture. I can well remember the first time—it was 1947 and I was living in Greenwich Village—that I heard the word *authentic* used in a purely pejorative sense. Anything authentic could be copied and, at the same time, smoothed out and made slick. Things authentic were raw and rough-edged. The supermarket soon replaced the farmers' market and the family grocery store. Same thing in the culture business.

The second great force for change, more powerful, in fact, than technology—for the shopkeepers of culture, for these folks, then and now, have been only casually interested in research and development, letting others take the real risks of invention, just as, in an artistic sense, the custodians of culture are not interested in the real risks of creation; they hire and fire the creative types—was the discovery that, under controlled conditions, inordinate (not merely excessive, but simply incredible) profits could be made. Here the risks were and are high. It is a breathless gamble, a crapshoot, but enough huge fortunes are made to make the risks not wholly irrational. It really started with the movies and got well underway during the Depression. While the rest of the nation suffered, Hollywood made some money.

Not a whole lot, because these first generation aliens (who might as well have been Aliens from Outer Space for all they knew or cared about things American, our cultural roots or traditions) were not secure enough to wish to call too much attention to themselves. That remained for the next generation. Meantime the Hollywood guys were on our side, more or less, during World War II. Partly because, with good reason, they didn't want the other side to win, and partly because win, lose, or draw, they didn't want to get drafted. They turned their business into a war industry and cranked out propaganda and entertainment, making some good money at the same time. It was here that the makers and purveyors of the new popular culture realized the power of propaganda, covert as well as explicit. And they have used their media for this purpose, with many a hidden agenda ever since.

They were beginning to earn a portion of the one reward they really could not generate or control on their own—respectability. For centuries, ever since the heyday of Rome, show business people had mostly and often legally been classified as standing well outside the normal hierarchies and patterns of society. They were, as the Elizabethans used to say, "masterless men."

One thing they had done that slowly but surely changed things in their favor was to create stars and the star system. The origin was merchandising, but the concept took hold and soon enough meant more than an aid to large-scale buying and selling.

Very soon in the game, given the right context, it became possible to create stars possessed of very little, if any, talent. Some had some talent and some didn't. Talent became, finally, irrelevant to stardom. So, soon enough, did other factors like character and integrity. Soon enough, the "true" character of a star was irrelevant also. This aspect of the star system has proved beneficial to the movers and shakers of the business who have never been noted for sterling character or integrity. By now the second and third generations have been able to step forward and become public figures themselves without risk or shame. Similarly, the star system has spread first to all other shapes and forms of show business and entertainment, but also into all other aspects of our lives including politics and the professions, all the arts and crafts.

We of my generation (born 1929), and the next two after that, have witnessed these things happening in our time, energized by the demonic power of television, which was only very briefly a genuine competitor and soon developed as just another part of the total package—movies, radio, television, records, publishing, sports, fashion, the news—all of it now, thanks to the fun and games of arbitrage and the irresistible impulse toward mergers, joined together in an indissoluble multinational matrimony. What all this means (among other things) is that popular culture, in these last wild years of this bloody and terrible century, is whatever they say it is, whatever choices they choose to allow us to exercise. It means, too, that the human scale and communal pleasures of popular culture—movies seen in a real picture palace, vaudeville shows, the music hall, burlesque—are gone for good. Rock concerts and the like, loosely based on the May Day or Nuremberg rallies, don't count, at least in the sense of offering the communal experience. If you want to see where we have come, what we are up to, just consider the last couple of presidential inaugurations.

What all this means is that it is no longer possible to avoid or escape the impact of the mass-produced popular culture. For a very few people in my generation it was, strictly speaking, possible to escape the experience. Not since then. There is no place on earth safely away from it. We cannot spare our children or grandchildren from its, at best, baleful influence.

Not long ago, critic Lee Lescase, writing in *The Wall Street Journal*, took serious note of some of the attitudes that link show business (Hollywood) with the government of our nation, hunkered down inside the beltway: "In other words the image is more important than the reality. In fact there doesn't have to be *any* reality. In a life revolving around prime time, events, even events involving thousands of people can be arranged solely for the cameras." Really? Take today's paper (*Washington Post*) for example. In the news section we have "As the World Watches on TV, Lorena Bobbitt's Trial Opens." In the "Style" section we learn that not many people, on the scene at least, seem to be as interested as the reporters: "Because so few members of the actual public turned out at the courthouse, the hundreds of journalists were reduced to interviewing T-shirt hawkers ($20 for a 'Love Hurts' shirt autographed by John Bobbitt, himself). . . ."

Years ago, in the 1950s, I worked for television as a writer for a show that died in labor. My first day on the job the producer told me the score: "If you think television has anything to do with art, you're crazy. If you think it's entertainment, you are naive and misinformed. Television is purely and simply an advertising medium (this long before the shopping network). Your job is purely and simply to write stuff to fill in the time and space between the ads." Years later I have to admit he spoke the truth. During the 1960s, and ever since, they took over the news and information services of television. Nothing has changed since then except that nobody even bothers to apologize any more for the wealth of misinformation and disinformation and nonsense they solemnly and relentlessly produce and present to us. No wonder that nothing can equal or even approach the contempt that the masters of popular culture feel for the audience they routinely abuse.

Nevertheless, even though they are desperately few and far between, there are real people and moments in the history of our popular culture that are worthwhile and worthy of honor. Fellini and his works are surely among these precious few. And you will have your own special favorites and examples, though I am willing to wager that in whatever field you choose to consider, from grand opera to Grand Old Opry, the honorable few will be very few. And they will be creators and performers, not the producers and dealers.

Dear George Garrett,

I was planning to write a letter to Christy Turlington, the supermodel (*it's all about models these days*), and tell her my thrilling life story and see if I can't, you know, like make friends. And I may even do that a little later. But right now I consider it my bounden duty to deal with you.

You certainly sound like a bitter and cynical little old man. Judging by this article of yours, which you in fact have not finished yet, there is no real popular culture in our country any more (if there ever was any), just a whole lot of mass-produced and packaged junk. Trash created by trash for trash on all sides and at all levels. Your not-so-subtle subtext seems to be that next to nothing is or can be immune from the AIDS-like viral infection of this *faux* pop culture foisted on us by degenerate and probably subhuman criminals and blatantly designed to appeal to our most bestial and atavistic promptings.

Am I right or am I wrong? Let your readers (if any) decide for themselves.

But before we get that far maybe I can talk you out of publishing this thing. Look, be sensible. You are no Saul Bellow or Philip Roth. That's for sure. You are not even an Updike or a Richard Ford. In the pop culture game of the literary you are a definite bench warmer. People will say, if they haven't already, that you are just sour and mean-spirited and even jealous of the others, writers like Jay McInerney and Norman Mailer who have earned their stars and wound stripes. They are legitimate public figures. You don't catch them saying bad things about the state of popular culture in America. They are very careful who they criticize. And so should you be.

But, for the sake of argument, let's say you really believe what you've been saying, which, basically, is that the world has gone crazy. So? You noticed that. It has happened in the last decade of every century we know anything about. Believe me, it won't last long. And on the other side of the great millennial divide there is plenty of profit for all, if we just wait patiently for our turn at the trough.

Meanwhile watch your step. Control yourself. The great thing about popular culture as it's practiced nowadays is that it is altogether disposable and utterly forgettable. If you can't stand Eddie Murphy or Beavis and Butthead, it doesn't matter. Something else, better or worse, the same and different, will be along before you can say Rumpelstiltskin.

Now I better finish this off right away. I don't want to keep my supermodel waiting.

All the best,

—John Towne

p.s.   You want a second opinion? You're ugly, too.

p.p.s. On second thought I think I'll write Kate Moss. Her cockney accent is cute and her belly button is wonderful. I think I may be in love again.

—J.T.

Stars and Bars:
A Confederate Collage

Though black hostility to Confederate totems lay relatively dormant for two decades after the civil rights struggles of the early 1960s, it resurfaced in the mid-1980s and has escalated ever since.

—Tony Horwitz, *Confederates in the Attic*

A cool, sun-rinsed early afternoon in London at the end of this past summer. My wife and I are strolling along Birdcage Walk, coming back from a visit to the National Portrait Gallery. Near Buckingham Palace, I notice the black bearskin hats and scarlet coats of the Old Guard, just relieved by the daily Changing of the Guard and coming home to Wellington Barracks. Even at the tag end of this ancient ceremony, with nobody much watching now, the Guards—perfectly aligned and dressed, arms swinging precisely together, the little bayonets on their formidable assault rifles glinting, shiny black hob-nailed boots hitting the pavement exactly together—look wonderful, justly the exemplary model for all the marching soldiers in the world.

Once upon a time a soldier myself, I pause and watch in silent awe as the Guard swings into position in front of the Barracks. Before they are dismissed from duty, there is one more detail, a vital one, to take care of. Escorts to the Colors (the regimental battle flag) form up and, while the rest of the Guard presents arms in salute, they quick-march to a doorway where the Colors are formally handed over to their counterparts on interior guard duty in the Barracks.

For more than a thousand years, until the early twentieth century (and do not forget the Iwo Jima Memorial of the Marine Corps or fail to note that a book about the six men who raised the flag in Iwo Jima, *Flags of Our Fathers,* has been high on *The New York Times* bestseller list for months), battle flags served various practical purposes in combat even as they were profoundly symbolic, representing not a nation and not any cause, but the identity and honor of a military unit. To carry the flag under fire was a high (if highly dangerous) honor; to guard it was an almost sacred duty; to capture it from an enemy was a great triumph.

I once served in an old cavalry regiment where some Confederate battle flags, taken in battle, were on display at headquarters. In Salisbury once I visited the museum of a defunct British regiment, one that (never mind the outcome of the war) had won major victories against my ancestors in the American Revolution and now had the battle flags to show for it. In the end, the Americans won that war. But the British regiment from Wiltshire had won its battles and brought home the proof of it.

⤜⟴⟅⤛

The topic—the Confederate battle flag and what it may mean to others and myself—is these days as delicate and dangerous (and proverbial) as a footpath through a mine field. To be walked with greatest care, on tiptoe as it were. To be talked about, yes, but with tact—that is, with an awareness of the feelings of others and allowing for the validity of some or all of those feelings even when one does not, cannot, share all of them without some serious reservations. One has to be honest and open in order to expect the same integrity from others. To be less than that, though perhaps typical in and of our hypocritical times, would be, among other things, simply condescending. Would be to ratify the already awkward situation in which, all too often and for all kinds of dubious reasons, we do not talk seriously to each other about any number of things that seriously matter to us. Would be to deny, if only tacitly, that there are many things at once unthinkable and unspeakable at the concealed and bitter heart of our social life.

Any survivor of the savage twentieth century is familiar with accepting the unacceptable, thinking the unthinkable, saying out loud what others may deem to be unspeakable.

It is not a serious challenge to the imagination to understand that the feelings of others may be very different from my own, that my assumptions are often alien to those of others. For example, I do not defend the right of any government, or indeed other quasi-official public institutions, to fly the Confederate battle flag. And I am more than a little uneasy at the personal use and display of the Confederate battle flag. (Or Old Glory, either, for that matter.) But, by the same token, I do not think that anyone has an inalienable right to remove those symbols unless and until those who wish to remove or expunge them have fully earned the power to do so both at the ballot box and in the courthouse.

Another basic assumption, personal, but not without wider implications, is this: that in the notorious and much-discussed case of the murder of Michael Westerman near Guthrie, Kentucky—an event often cited and studied by hotheads, white and black, to advance their own agendas—the serious attempt by the defense lawyers to mitigate the gravity of the crime because Westerman's pickup was flying a Confederate battle flag is an unacceptable absurdity.

⋯⊷⊜ ⊜⊶⋯

The Civil War, its battles and battle flags included, remains (it seems) urgently interesting to a large number of readers. Recently, for *The Sewanee Review* (Spring 2000), I set out, innocently and ignorantly, to write a chronicle-essay-review of some of the newer and representative books about the Civil War. This sampling of general and particular histories, biographies, letters, diaries, cartoons, photographs, and works of fiction for adults and children, added thirty-one titles to the already "more than 50,000 books written about the war—at the rate of a book published a day for every day since the war ended," in the words of historian J. Tracy Power. At this writing (fall 2000), I find that our local Barnes and Noble superstore has an entire display table of several dozen new Civil War books, all of them published since my piece in *The Sewanee Review* went to press. Turning back to a recent issue of *The New York Times Book Review* (August 20, 2000), I note a full-page review of three brand new novels about Ulysses S. Grant. "Three novels about Ulysses S. Grant?" the reviewer, Dante Ramos, writes. "Why the sudden fuss? Well, it may simply be that the public's interest in the Civil War is once again on the rise, to judge from the resurgent debate on the use of the Confederate battle flag."

Call it an unanticipated spin-off from the controversy. Where else could this troubling quarrel be so deftly transformed into a matter of marketing and commerce?

Is this a great country or what?

⟶━◉╺━⟵

When I was growing up in the Great Depression, there were, believe it or not, no bumper stickers yet nor clothing sold or worn with commercial brand name advertisements or personal statements displayed. Cars were just beginning to be sold with the dealers' names prominently shown. In those days, too, flags had their proper places. Flags were not to be taken lightly. The law of the land was that desecration of an American or a state flag was a crime. A generation later, in the 1960s, flags of all kinds could be legally burned or destroyed, used for commerce or as colorful decoration.

I can remember seeing battle flags of various kinds, including Confederate ones, on display in museums and chapels. I remember the little flags, including the Confederate one, stuck into the soft earth alongside small, uniform tombstones, rows and rows of them, on the occasion of various national and local holidays. I can well remember veterans of the Civil War, some of them my blood kinfolk and all of them very old, who were honored even as they, in turn, honored their fallen comrades and fallen enemies.

The Civil War killed too many and went on much too long. In its ratio of casualties to population, it remains by far the worst war in our history. According to Shelby Foote in *The Civil War*, "the butcher's bill" included one out of ten of all the Union's able-bodied men aged eighteen to sixty-five and one out of four of the Confederate male population. It needs to be understood that this is a far worse ratio than, for example, France and Britain in

World War I, than Germany or the Soviet Union in World War II.

Rivers of blood. Acres of amputated arms and legs. A generation of cripples.

(For those interested in the novel idea of reparations, what sort of monetary value would you be prepared to set on all those spent and wasted lives?)

The war lasted much longer than it might have, more than it should have. Still, it could easily have lasted even longer if the Confederates had elected to fight to the last man or to wage a guerrilla war. General Sherman feared that possibility and wrote a letter to Grant of April 25th, 1865:

> No surrender of an army not actually at the mercy of an antagonist, was ever made without "terms," and these always define the military status of the surrendered. . . . I now apprehend that the Rebel Armies will disperse; and instead of dealing with six or seven states, we will have to deal with numberless bands of desperadoes headed by such men as Mosby, Forrest, Red Jackson, & others who know not, and care not for danger and its consequences.

Lee and Johnston, Kirby-Smith and Bedford Forrest, briefly considered that idea and dismissed it. In that sense the whole nation, the Union, owes a debt to the Confederate military leaders for choosing the way of formal and honorable surrender, thus, at the least, saving many thousands of lives on both sides.

The Civil War offered the bloodiest and most sustained period of combat ever faced by any American forces before or since. From the experience of our bloody twentieth century we, or anyway the many veterans still among us, know how it is possible, even likely, that men on both sides, sharing the honors of combat, develop a special respect for each other. In the absence of a pattern of horrid atrocities, as was the case in the Pacific battles in World War II, combat soldiers tend to honor the skill and courage of fellow soldiers. Oliver Wendell Holmes spoke explicitly of this at his 1884 regimental reunion in Keene, New Hampshire: "You could not stand up day after day, in those indecisive contests where overwhelming victory was impossible because neither side would run as they ought to when beaten, without getting at least something of the same brotherhood for the enemy that the north pole of a magnet has for the south, each working in an opposite sense to the other, but unable to get along without the other."

And there is yet another lesson learned from the experience of combat and accurately described by Paul Fussell in his memoir *Doing Battle*: "Combat makes you realize how unspeakably lucky you are to have lost, as yet, no limbs, to eat and sleep daily, and to be on the winning side."

What if . . . ?

What if, after the first terrible battles demonstrated beyond any doubt that the Civil War was going to be a slaughterhouse, both sides had seriously attempted to negotiate a solution?

What if Lincoln (and Jefferson Davis) had been dedicated, in the modern sense, to some kind of a "peace process"?

Would the results have been better or worse?

Discuss.

⊷⇒◯⇐⊷

Like many Southerners, I had family on both sides in the
Civil War. Not counting a network of cousins and such,
I had four great-grandfathers and one grandfather in the
war. I have some vivid memories of some of these old
men. Two were dedicated abolitionists, though only one
fought for the Union, and he was also the only one who
kept a diary of it. Colonel Oliver Hazard Palmer was the
commanding officer of the 108th New York Volunteers.
Here he is describing the battle of Fredericksburg in
December 1862 in terms that might remind a modern
reader of the D-day landing in *Saving Private Ryan*:

> I remained on the field until nearly dark and until the
> fighting of the day was mainly over. It was a terribly
> hot place. The shells were flying in every direction and
> plowing up the earth all around me all over as though
> in a whirlwind. The scene was frightful but intensely
> exciting. New Brigades of fresh troops were forming
> in line and advancing hoping to be more successful, but
> I knew they were doomed to disappointment and
> death. Broken & shattered Companies, Regiments &
> Brigades were falling back. Dead and wounded
> officers & men were being borne to the rear, some in
> blankets, some on the shoulders of comrades. You
> would see one here with one arm, another there with
> one leg trying to get back. Some moaning, some
> swearing, occasionally a poor fellow trying to save the
> half not shot away would disappear in fragments by a
> solid shot or amidst the smoke of an exploding shell.
> . . . At sundown I made my way to town to gather up
> fragments of my Brigade not knowing what the next
> day might require. Out of the 1,200 men in my

command in the morning I could get together at night only 400. It was a sorry sight.

Later, in a farewell speech to his regiment, Colonel Palmer stressed the honor and meaning of the unit's battle flags: "Remember that I own an interest in those once bright and beautiful, now scarred and tattered but still more beautiful banners, which I value above all price. They bear the record of your valor. The three score and ten stars made in them by Rebel bullets at the battle of Antietam form a constellation worthy almost of adoration."

⋆⟹ ⟸⋆

I have always thought "Dixie" one of the best tunes I ever heard. Our adversaries over the way attempted to appropriate it, but I insisted yesterday that we fairly captured it. . . . I now request the band to favor me with its performance.

—Abraham Lincoln, 10 April 1865

⋆⟹ ⟸⋆

In the second half of the twentieth century (and continuing into this new one) our society has developed the capacity to trivialize and vulgarize almost anything, sacred and profane alike. The Civil War, with its totems, artifacts, and symbols (and, indeed, its pure and simple facts), is not immune. "Virtual reality" has by now become hopelessly confused with reality. We are living in an age of reenactments, including elaborate replays of Civil War battles from which the dead rise up and the wounded wipe away their painless scars.

Thus arises a final question, not to be answered here and maybe, after all, not to be answered at all: Is this controversy about the flying and flaunting of the Confederate battle flag (and the playing of "Dixie" and the public portraits of and monuments to slave-owning Confederate heroes) a matter of "real" debate or is it merely a minor piece in the complex and confrontational chess game of race and politics in contemporary America?

False Confessions

The author of this story had other plans for me. In his, alas, typical ignorance and ineptitude, he decided to use me (one more time!) as the heavy, a really bad guy in a bleak and downbeat story that most likely would gross you out or, in any case, would sure enough give you the willies, as they say, troubled about the essential nature of humankind as represented, exemplified by me, an anti-hero if there ever was one.

You probably don't know me from Adam or Adam's Rottweiler. And I can't blame you for that. How would you know me, and why would you? I ask you! I don't intend to bother you, to cover the whole thing. All you really need to know at this point is that I am precisely what I seem to be (how many of you can make that claim?)—a fictional character, another imaginary person who usually ends up doing and being whatever some author, real or so-called, wants the aforesaid character (usually no more substantial or dimensional than a shadow) to do or to be.

There are, of course, many disadvantages to life (and death) as a fictional character. I could go on and on about the subject and soon generate overwhelming ennui all around. But you can easily imagine most of the pains and problems and disappointments. Not least of which is the almost complete absence of free will. Whether I am willing to admit it or not, most of the time I have to be what my author wants. More to the point I have to be and to do what he wants even when it challenges common credibility and violates the sacred and sanctified rules and guiding principles of literary criticism. Which means (think about it; go figure) I not only can't save myself, but also I can't come to his aid, either. I end up having to take the blame, together with my author, for whatever he makes me do or leave undone. That is really and truly unfair. And note the irony of it: I am composed, in fact and in any fiction I find myself involved in, of the figments and fragments of his conscious and unconscious obsessions. He may well think that he is freer than I am. If so, that is purely and simply a delusion.

It would be funny if it weren't so damn personal.

I said chances are you have never heard of me. Fine, I never heard of you, either. (In a culture firmly based on celebrity, that puts us both at a distinct disadvantage.) I never claimed to be a Captain Ahab or a Huck Finn, not Bech or Rabbit Angstrom or Zuckerman, either. My name is John Towne, and I have "starred" as the (pardon the expression) protagonist in maybe half a dozen short stories as well as in the widely reviewed and yet little-known novel *Poison Pen*. Most of the people who reviewed that book found something or other nice to say about the author, but they seldom, if ever, spoke or speak well or kindly and gently of me. *The New York Times Book Review* called me "a low-life crank"; "a lecherous, misanthropic failed academic," opined *The Chicago Tribune;* someone writing for *The Village Voice* called me "an exceptionally sleazy picaro." And on and on in that vein. Probably the strongest and meanest judgment (it would be slander if I were real) appeared in *The Greensboro News* in a review by Fred Chappell, who identified me as "a loathsome, racist, sexist, crude, and gruesome creep."

Meanwhile the author who invented me was being described in other terms. Here is how *The New York Times Book Review* elected to characterize him: "He is a well-respected writer with a prestigious academic position—he's Henry Hoyns Professor of Creative Writing at the University of Virginia."

Bully for him! Pushing seventy, he makes about as much as a junior corporate executive fresh out of college.

Do you know what he originally had in mind for me in this story? He planned to put me back into an academic setting and context (where I have done hard time before—"an academic gypsy and con man," *The Roanoke Times* named me) so that I could be poorer than he is. He planned to involve me and expose me in a singularly repellent story. It tells how I set out to seduce and betray the wife of a friend and colleague of mine, a poor old guy who is suffering from Alzheimer's. My motivation, such as it was (my author not planning to go too deep into the subtleties of motivation), at least at the outset: revenge. I want to hurt him because I did not get the promotion (and tenure) that I talked myself into believing that I richly deserved, even though I had not done anything to earn it and even though he, alone, among the entire senior faculty, had always been generous and friendly to me and was probably the only member of the whole frigging department who thought I had any redeeming social value and who would have spoken up for me if he hadn't already been diagnosed with Alzheimer's.

In the story, according to the author, he, this suffering and slowly dying professor, was the scapegoat I invented. None of the others was particularly vulnerable, and, anyway, they wouldn't let me close enough to do them any harm.

Another motivation the author laid on me was that

the wife in question was really good-looking. Extraordinary. Exceptionally attractive. I was to observe and/or remark, somewhere in the story, that except for her golden hair she was a first-rate knockoff of Cindy Crawford. (That would serve to characterize me as a guy who took popular culture a little too seriously, at face value. Which, in fact, is true.) This second motivation, lust, would tend to add to the ambiguity of my situation: that I was using the payback motive to disguise the simpler truth from myself and to justify my strong urge to try to seduce his wife while he was altogether defenseless and she was more or less vulnerable.

Another reason that the author planned to motivate me by sexual desire was that he had used this same thing, in other stories and in *Poison Pen*, to explain away my actions. Problem is, this kind of evidence is inadmissible and irrelevant. What I may have done or left undone in the context of another story has no bearing on this one.

What was supposed to happen here was that I would gently insinuate myself into her good graces by helping them in any and all ways that I possibly could—running errands for her, taking care of minor tasks and chores, and baby-sitting the old fart for a few hours while she went off, like a good creative faculty wife, to paint pictures or write poems or throw pots or whatever.

In the story the seduction turns out to be a whole lot easier than it probably would be—for you or for me or for anyone else—in real life. Pretty soon I am regularly having fun and games with her anywhere and anytime I can. Sometimes even right there in the house, in their bedroom. I mean, he has reached the point where he can't remember from one minute to the next; so what do we care if he should walk in on us? And it is all great and wonderful, and I find myself enjoying every minute of it.

The author adds some complexity to my motivation by asserting that, in part, I am also getting even with all the beautiful women who have turned me down and/or spurned my amorous advances in a lifetime spent trying to score. Well, he is way off base there. By and large I have never had any problem making out with women, plain or fancy. I like women a lot, and most of the time I know how to get along with them. And that important and undeniable fact does not come across in the story. Let the author say whatever he pleases. My overall record speaks for itself.

What happens to me in the story, as the author sees it, is that I will inevitably fall in love with the woman. I don't mean to, of course (whoever does?), but I can't help myself, and I do so, anyway. And then because I have begun to care for her, I also begin to feel profoundly guilty. Meanwhile, though I am not aware of it yet, she also is tormented with guilt. So there you are with the three of us—the two guilt-ridden lovers and the old guy who has passed beyond all that kind of pain and trouble. Now then. You know, and I know, and I suspect even my author does, that most of the time guilt leads nowhere else but to a lot of deeper trouble. When we are feeling really guilty, we quickly discover that we are unable to forgive ourselves. So our first thought is always to unload that guilt onto somebody else, anybody who happens to be handy. As far as I can tell, guilt (not shame, mind you, or sorrow) does nobody any good. Except maybe psychiatrists.

In this particular story that we are talking about, there is a big scene, après some very good and memorable afternoon sex, during which we each try to assuage our guilt with false confessions. I intend to tell the truth, but only a part of it. I don't tell her that I have come to love her. I tell her that the whole thing was just about getting even with her husband and that now that I have done just that, I feel wonderful.

Fighting back with fury, she says the whole thing is truly funny. Because, you see, she never really loved her husband or cared about him one way or another while he was still well and wide awake. She wanted comfort and security, and she got just that. But when he became ill, she cared for him out of guilt. All the time she was ready, willing, and able to be seduced by anybody, the first man who came along. Which happened to be me, but might as well have been the postman.

It's a joke on both of us, she would say, ha-ha. I was not to be allowed to take any pride or pleasure in my seduction of her. And all of my guilt, real or imaginary, was utterly without meaning or implication.

On the way out of the house (why am I described as tiptoeing, for Christ's sake?) I decide to steal something valuable from him. My first thought is his real nice, expensive wristwatch. I could take it right off his arm if I wanted to, and he would never know the difference. But then, instead, the souvenir I take is his Mont Blanc fountain pen, resting on his dusty desk. I mean, why not? He won't be writing anything with it, anyway.

Then the way the story ends is that, even before the academic year is over and done with, the old guy dies. His young wife (did I fail to mention that fact—young? Sorry) puts him in the ground at the old college cemetery. The only plots left available are down at the far end close-by the railroad tracks. Well, at least he can listen to the whistle and rattle of freight trains coming and going. Eternity could be a lot worse.

After the funeral she packs up and takes off. I like to think she has gone to Southern California or Florida or maybe the Gulf Coast. Maybe Mexico. Someplace warm, anyway, where she can stretch out on a beach blanket and show off her incredible figure and pick up or ignore any old geezer she wants to.

I like to think that she sometimes thinks of me.

I am portrayed as thinking these things because I am busy packing up my own stuff to move on to the only job I have been able to get—at a college in miserable upstate New York, Joyce Carol Oates territory, Frederick Busch turf. I will freeze my ass off up there where it stays dark more than half the time.

The reader will think that this serves me right.

In the last couple of lines the reader will also think that this story, in the form of a confession, is presumed to have been written with my newly acquired Mont Blanc pen. Here, at the tag end, I am shown wondering whether or not I will ever write her a letter and what I will find to say in it, assuming I can find out where she has gone.

Even though the author insists he is going through a "dark" period and can't help himself, I find this story to be too downbeat. I would much rather not be caught up in something so ugly and offensive and heavy-handed. Of course, it is only a slight variation on the familiar and conventional plot in which somebody sets out—on a bet or an impulse, out of anger or frustration or boredom—to seduce somebody else and, either in success or failure, falls in love. The odd little moral of such tales, usually, is the commonplace truth that sometimes there are good consequences of bad actions. Well, that's not news. All of us know that much.

Admittedly we have only had time to deal with the general story line here. As my author would be the first to point out, we have neglected to consider the texture and the details, the little things he likes to do that, ideally, add up. Like, for example, plotting the pen very early in the story in a brisk, almost casual description of the professor's desk and study. I would notice and admire the pen, among other valuable things, that's all. But it would seem like an old friend when I suddenly decide to steal it. And I have to admit he does a nice little thing with her beautiful blonde hair, touched and glowing in the late afternoon sun, on the blue pillowcase just before he (I) offers up his confession. Now I wouldn't say that my author is completely without any talent. Imagine how that would be for the poor, helpless (pardon) protagonist, prisoner of a complete, no-talent, bumbling fool! There are plenty of those out there. And so it is that even if we are not dealing with an Updike or a Roth or any such, I can nevertheless count my blessings. It can always be a whole lot worse, believe me.

One of the great flaws of the story, as the author wrote it, disregarding my advice, is that he doesn't spend much time or detail on the professor. The story would have more meaning and impact if we had some special sympathy for the old guy. There was a brief scene, later cut during revision, in which we see the professor, with my help and the help of his wife, get dressed to go and teach a class. Which, of course, he can't do, anyway. But there is this little game of getting him ready to go forth into the world and to do something. Only by the time he's ready to go, he has forgotten what it is he was planning to do. The author almost stumbled onto something worthwhile when he decided that the old guy had wonderful clothes and that he looked good in them. We get him dressed; he admires himself in the mirror; and then he wanders around the house, upstairs and down, basement and attic, without rhyme or reason, vaguely wondering what is happening to him. But the author chickened out of that scene.

I could be disloyal and tell you a thing or two about the author, things he would just as soon you didn't know,

now and forever. But what good would that do me? Seriously, that is the first and foremost question that you have to ask of anybody, especially including fictional characters. What is in it for him/her? From the school of experience I can tell you that people, human beings, don't do anything either good or evil without there being something—pride, pleasure, vanity, self-esteem—in it for themselves. Even the purest forms of altruism and sacrifice are tainted. (Know what I mean?) Love, I guess, true love is the coincidental state, the odd and unexpected occasion when the lives and the circuitry of the desires of two people (briefly, briefly) come together and share the same frequency or wavelength. Or else, like happiness, love can be defined as the state of being well-deceived.

What I really hate, though, is being made the public scapegoat for the author's guilt. He heaps troubles on my head in hopes of hiding the grubby truth about himself. You can bet your sweet ass he has done plenty of things (thought, word, and deed) that he ought to be sorry for.

In the various and sundry fictions I have lived in and through, I have been allowed to be happy a few times. And I was even happy at times in this otherwise unhappy story up until, but including, that afternoon. Her beautiful blonde hair splashed on the blue pillow. Dust motes dancing in sunlight, the sweet smell and the smooth touch of her. Taste of her still on the tip of my tongue. Even the sound of her voice as she came to curse my name. And myself, ageless and weightless, floating in time as if in flowing water, for once fully satisfied and, for that moment, feeling free. Free at last to tell the truth, to confess all and maybe be forgiven. Which turned out to be exactly what the author had planned for me all along.

Author of thirty-two books and editor or coeditor of nineteen others, George Garrett earned both undergraduate and graduate degrees at Princeton and recently retired from the University of Virginia after a forty-year teaching career. Among his honors and awards are the Rome Prize of the American Academy of Arts and Letters, a *Sewanee Review* Fellowship in Poetry, fellowships from the Guggenheim, Ford, and Rockefeller Foundations and the National Endowment for the Arts, the T. S. Eliot Award of the Ingersoll Foundation, the Aiken Taylor Award for Modern American Poetry, the PEN/Malamud Award for Excellence in Short Fiction, and an Award in Literature from the American Academy of Arts and Letters. Together with his wife of fifty years, he lives in Charlottesville, Virginia.

Jeb Livingood is a graduate of the University of Virginia's M.F.A. Program in Creative Writing, where he currently serves as faculty advisor for *Meridian*, a semiannual literary magazine. His fiction and nonfiction have appeared in *Best New American Voices 2001* (Harcourt), *The Texas Review*, *Yemassee*, *The Hollins Critic*, and *C-ville*.